CW00522289

Motion Graphics

Fairchild Books

An imprint of Bloomsbury Publishing Plc

Imprint previously known as AVA Publishing

50 Bedford Square	1385 Broadway
London	New York
WC1B 3DP	NY 10018
UK	USA

www.bloomsbury.com

**FAIRCHILD BOOKS, BLOOMSBURY and the Diana logo are trademarks
of Bloomsbury Publishing Plc**

© Bloomsbury Publishing Plc, 2016

Ian Crook and Peter Beare have asserted their right under the Copyright,
Designs and Patents Act, 1988, to be identified as Authors of this work.

All rights reserved. No part of this publication may be reproduced or
transmitted in any form or by any means, electronic or mechanical,
including photocopying, recording, or any information storage or
retrieval system, without prior permission in writing from the publishers.

No responsibility for loss caused to any individual or organization acting
on or refraining from action as a result of the material in this publication
can be accepted by Bloomsbury or the author.

British Library Cataloguing-in-Publication Data
A catalogue record for this book is available from the British Library.

ISBN: PB: 978-1-4725-6900-4
            ePDF: 978-1-4725-6901-1

Library of Congress Cataloging-in-Publication Data
Beare, Peter, 1970-
Motion graphics : principles and practices from the ground up /
Peter Beare and Ian Crook.
        pages cm
Includes bibliographical references and index.
ISBN 978-1-4725-6900-4 (alk. paper)—ISBN 978-1-4725-6901-1
(alk. paper) 1. Computer animation. 2. Multimedia systems.
I. Crook, Ian. II. Title.
TR897.7.B38 2015
777'.7—dc23
2014046639

Typeset by Roger Fawcett-Tang
Printed and bound in China

Motion Graphics
Principles and Practices
from the Ground Up

Ian Crook and Peter Beare

Fairchild Books
An imprint of Bloomsbury Publishing Plc

B L O O M S B U R Y
LONDON · NEW DELHI · NEW YORK · SYDNEY

CONTENTS

INTRODUCTION

In today's visually rich, digitally connected world, a viewer cannot watch TV, view a film screening at a cinema, or browse the Internet without being bombarded by motion graphics. This book aims to act as a primer in the world of motion graphics regardless of your area of expertise. It aims to provide you with a wide understanding of the discipline and a familiarity with the core principles, concepts, and terminology.

The book is structured into two parts. The first part introduces the "toolset" that a practitioner of motion graphics needs from the outset as well as a series of core concepts that underpin the skills and principles of graphic production and motion graphic design.

The second part consists of a detailed examination of the motion graphics design process and workflow for both sole producers and members of larger production teams.

Interspersed throughout is a series of case studies that provides insight into the real-life experience of motion graphic experts as well as practical exercises for you to try yourself.

The aim of the book is not to teach you everything that could be learned about one or two software tools. Instead, it is our intention that you recognize the scope of expertise that motion graphic designers possess. This expertise extends beyond competence with industry-standard tools, and includes softer skills, such as imagination, analysis, discipline, and a desire to work with others. This is not a how-to book; rather, it is a "what-do-I-need-to-think-about" book.

Luther

The title sequence made by Momoco for the BBC series *Luther* uses a richly colored and highly textured background with gritty silhouettes to offset stark white lettering expertly setting the tone for the drama to come.

www.momoco.co.uk

Strike Suit Zero

Motion graphics specialists Territory produced in-game display overlays, cinematic sequences, and a release trailer for the game *Strike Suit Zero*. The graphics serve a dual purpose of providing valuable technical and contextual information to enable the player to play the game, as well as providing an immersive and captivating experience to enhance the believability of the world.

www.territorystudio.com

WHO IS THIS BOOK FOR?

A silhouetted figure falls gracefully between skyscrapers displaying advertising imagery. Words fly across the screen spelling out the lyrics of a song. A globe spins and zooms into a war-torn country. Money rises from the screen to explain an economic situation.

These are typical examples of the kind of moving imagery that pervade our media culture. Now, more than ever, we are surrounded by motion graphics on our TVs and cinema screens; on our phones, computers, and tablets; on Main Street; and in our galleries.

The concept of moving pictures is not new; people have been producing animated drawings of one form or another since the late nineteenth century. What is new, however, is the growth of techniques, assisted by technology, that have enabled producers to create ever more creative examples.

The realm of motion graphics crosses many disciplines—from animation to graphic design, to video and film production, to visual effects.

Our aim is to provide you with a wide understanding of the discipline of motion graphics and to ensure you have a familiarity with the core principles, concepts, and terminology.

The book aims to be:

- an essential toolkit, providing information for consideration when planning and creating motion graphic projects

- an exercise book, challenging you to develop creative motion graphics through interactive exercises

- a guide, showing how established designers have developed and incorporated the moving image in their projects

- a resource, giving you access to wider sources of information through a dedicated website (www.bloomsbury.com/crook-motion-graphics)

- a manifesto, encouraging you to implement creativity from the outset

Killzone overlays

Sony Entertainment Corporation's game series *Killzone* features a selection of cut scenes and Head Up Display overlays developed by Territory. These provide additional information that allows the players to have a fuller interactive experience and deeper emotional connection with the story.

www.territorystudio.com

WHAT IS MOTION GRAPHICS?

The actual definition of motion graphics is at once extremely simple and impossible to pin down. Simply put, motion graphics encompasses movement, rotation, or scaling of images, video, and text over time on screen, usually accompanied by a soundtrack (e.g., voice-over, music).

This simple definition, however, only describes the mechanism, the actual physical process. It is like defining a cake by describing the recipe. It does not really convey the scale and scope of what is generally considered to be motion graphics, nor does it clearly differentiate motion graphics from other forms of media such as animation or visual effects.

The term *motion graphics* was probably derived from motion graphic design and so shares many similarities with the graphic design discipline. One of the first instances of the use of the name was by the American animator John Whitney (1917–1995), often considered the father of computer animation, when in 1960 he set up his company Motion Graphics Incorporated to produce TV advertisements and title sequences using a computer of his own devising.

As a result of this graphic design background, motion graphics tend to use simplification and abstraction, reducing an image down to a diagrammatic form. This does not mean, however, that motion graphics cannot use other graphical elements. Any visual element—text, image, texture, shape, or line—is suitable to be part of a motion graphic.

The term *motion* itself is also somewhat misleading. An object that appears and disappears in the same position on a screen may not be described as moving; however, it is animated. Therefore, the characteristics of a motion graphic are based on time as well as movement. As a **motionographer** it is your job to design and coordinate this animation.

The defining point of a motion graphic is that it has the purpose of communication rather than simply being a viewing experience. It is an extra layer of information that helps to explain a point or concept. A motion graphic is instrumental in communicating something as simple as the title to a program or as complex as the working of a machine.

Thus we arrive at a definition of motion graphics:

"The choreography of graphical elements over time to convey information."

TIP It may help to consider some of the places and situations that motion graphics are typically seen:

- film and TV title sequences
- TV advertising
- news and station identifications
- infographics
- music videos
- business presentations
- educational presentations
- websites
- DVD and Blu-ray menus
- art galleries
- clubs and events

RSA Animate by Cognitive

The RSA Animate series, created by Cognitive, typifies what can be accomplished by motion graphics. In the short videos, audio lectures are illustrated by high-speed cartoon drawings, which emerge on an infinite whiteboard canvas. The complex topics under discussion range from economic theory to social behavior, but the moving graphics enhance the spoken words by creating emphasis and assisting understanding and memory.

www.thersa.org/animate
www.wearecognitive.com

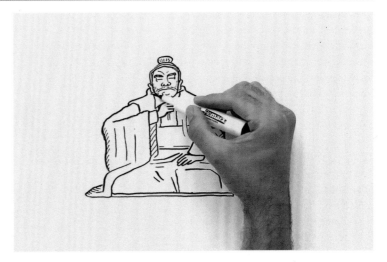

WHAT IS THE DIFFERENCE BETWEEN MOTION GRAPHICS AND ANIMATION?

We have seen that moving objects around on screen accompanied by a soundtrack is considered to be motion graphics, however this could also just as easily be a description of *animation*. When we laugh as modeling clay performs in the guise of Aardman's *Wallace & Gromit*; or are enchanted by the flat simplicity of Astley, Baker, and Davies' *Peppa Pig*; or are astounded by the pixel antics of Pixar's Buzz and Woody in *Toy Story*, we suspend belief that what we are watching is not real. We forget that it is all artifice, that it has been created. We are drawn into the story, the characters, and the emotion on display.

But it is still human-made objects moving around on screen accompanied by a soundtrack. So how can we differentiate it from motion graphics?

The key to the difference is purpose. An animated film's key purpose is to engage and entertain. It may contain a meaning or message, but there is an implicit understanding that the viewing experience is in some way enjoyable.

A motion graphic, on the other hand, may be constructed using the same tools and methods, but its primary purpose is to add meaning to something else. It could be engaging and entertaining, but first and foremost it is informative.

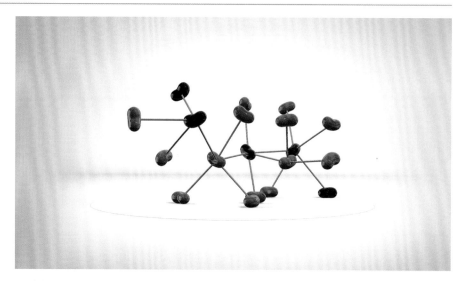

We should remember that while animation emerged from the discipline of illustration, motion graphics comes from the discipline of graphic design, and as such is meant to communicate information and visual design rather than emotional connection.

That is not to say that a piece of motion graphics could not contain characters or be emotionally moving; however, the primary motivation of a piece of motion graphics is visual communication.

ChilliBean

Chillibean supports the TV industry by providing services in video transcoding and large file transfer. Bark and Bite used the visual metaphor of beans in order to demonstrate how valuable media can be efficiently compressed and securely transferred around the world—a prime example of how motion graphics can help simplify technical information.

www.barkandbite.com

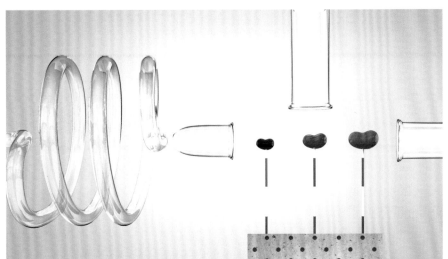

WHAT IS THE DIFFERENCE BETWEEN MOTION GRAPHICS AND VISUAL EFFECTS?

We have already established that it's difficult to pin down a definition of what motion graphics actually is. We can accept that on one level it is the animated movement of visual objects on a screen to the accompaniment of a soundtrack. We have seen that unlike animation it is not motivated by emotional engagement but rather by visual communication. This brings us to the next comparison, the difference between motion graphics and *visual effects* (commonly referred to as **VFX**).

Visual effects are generally visual elements added to video or film footage in such a way that the join or composite is invisible. The new element is incorporated in an entirely believable fashion so that the viewer will accept the addition as part of the filmed world. The added element may be a static image, such as a building or some signage, or may be an animated piece, such as a character or a vehicle. In order for the composite to be believable the new addition must move in tandem with the underlying footage. If the original camera wobbles around, the new element has to wobble accordingly, giving the impression that it is part of the same scene. The new element may be something fantastical like a robot, an alien, or a dinosaur, but the primary goal of the visual effects artist is integrated, believable acceptance.

Motion graphics differs here in that the primary goal is not integrated believability, but visual communication. The motion graphic element may be composited into some underlying footage but it is always separate. It is *in* the world of the footage, but not part of it.

An example may be where a motion graphic element is produced and overlaid onto some footage to further explain or give context to the filmed material. The new graphical elements are added to the footage so that they follow some part of it, using a technique known as motion tracking. As the footage moves, the motion graphic element moves too; however, it is always separate from the footage. The viewer will perceive it as an addition or overlay. They will not accept that it is part of the original filmed material.

A common technique that is often used by both motion graphics artists and visual effects artists is the use of *particle generators*. These are software simulations of particles that are emitted from a point with real world effects, such as gravity and wind, applied so that the particles are affected and altered. Variations of the effect could be used to create smoke, fire, dust, sparks, or any group of objects that move or flock in a natural manner.

In the world of VFX particle generators are often used to add virtual natural effects that would have been difficult or dangerous to film in reality. In the world of motion graphics, these effects are applied as a creation in their own right and used as visual decoration.

As with animation, there is crossover between motion graphics and visual effects. It can be difficult to separate one from the other. The guiding principle, however, is to ask yourself if the effect is an integral part of the footage, indistinguishable from the real world, in which case is it a visual effect; or if it is an effect purely in its own right, in which case it can be classified as a motion graphic.

Of course, to further add confusion, a motion graphic could be integrated into a scene seamlessly, for example, as some content on a screen. In this case the screen content would be considered the realm of the motion graphic artist, whereas the integration into the footage would be the realm of the visual effects artist. The two would work together to produce the final result.

Hannibal

Title sequences do more than provide textual information to identify the cast and crew. They do not simply captivate us with aimless spectacle. Exemplary title sequences establish the style, genre, and themes of the film or show; they may also foreshadow narrative information in order to create intrigue.

Many viewers of the NBC program *Hannibal* will be familiar with the eponymous Dr. Lecter. The title sequence by Momoco incorporates stunning special effects to playfully reference his appetite for fine wine and cannibalism.

www.momoco.co.uk

CHAPTER ONE
CONCEPTS:
TOOLS

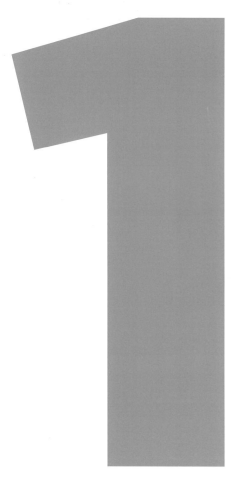

A tool is an intuitive device, the perfect appliance to assist with a very specific task. Its form and function are so intuitively connected that we would never consider using an alternative, and we would never have to ask for operating instructions.

By contrast, *technology* is a word used to describe an emerging or specialized device, an instrument that demands a degree of knowledge in order to operate that has not yet become so ubiquitous and dependable that it is second nature to understand. Alternatively, technology may describe something crucial, yet so entrenched and so complex, that its methods and value are mysterious to us.

In this chapter, we consider the characteristics of familiar tools. We will also consider the opportunities afforded by novel or emerging technologies, and demystify some of the underlying complexities of moving images.

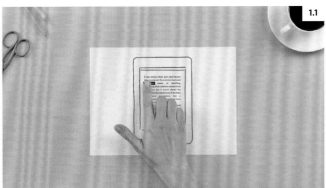

1.1 Kindle White

A commercial for Amazon's Kindle White, made by Troublemakers. The film reveals that reliance on CGI and digital animation tools is not mandatory or necessary.

Director Lucas Zanotto made use of inventive, colorful paper puppetry to vividly demonstrate the functionality of the eReader device.

http://troublemakers.tv/en
www.lucaszanotto.com

THE CAMERA

The earliest cameras were darkened rooms with a tiny opening in a window through which rays of light would pass in order to be projected on an opposing wall (the word *camera* is actually derived from the Latin for "darkened room": *camera obscura*).

Later, smaller, portable devices were developed: darkened boxes with lenses and mirrors that projected the image onto a small viewfinder. These had no permanent recording media, but they were useful aids for artists who could trace the projected image to accurately capture and study perspective.

It was the discovery of photographic principles that ultimately led to the sophisticated technologies for permanently recording still and moving images that we use today. But despite over a century of advances in photography, even the most modern cameras have inherited several core characteristics that were also features of their ancestors.

Focal length

The *lens* is a piece of shaped glass or transparent plastic that refracts light into the camera so that it can reach the film or sensor.

When light rays pass through the lens, the rays of light are refracted (i.e., bent inward) and converge to focus at a set distance from the lens, called the *focal plane*. The distance between the lens and the focal plane is called the *focal length*, and is measured in millimeters. Different focal lengths create images that have different angles of view on a scene, so a short focal length results in an image in which perspective and depth appear to be exaggerated, and a long focal length "flattens" an image so that distant objects seem much closer. We are probably more familiar with broader categories of lens type: wide-angle lenses (a short focal length, less than 50mm) and telephoto lenses (a long focal length, 50mm and higher).

Lenses can be categorized into two types in relation to their focal length. *Prime lenses* have a focal length of a fixed distance. *Zoom lenses* have a focal length that can be changed.

1.2–1.3 Wide angle versus telephoto
In both images, the performer holds an ID card toward the camera at arm's length. In the wide-angle version (1.2), the card appears to be larger because the wide-angle lens has the effect of exaggerating perspective and depth.

1.2

1.3

THE
CAMERA

VIDEO IMAGE
FORMATS

VIDEO
COMPRESSION
AND CODECS

STILL IMAGE
FORMATS

SOFTWARE

IMAGE
CREATION

IMAGE
MANIPULATION

TRADITIONAL
ART
MATERIALS

ALTERNATIVE
TOOLS

CASE STUDY:
MOMOCO

EXERCISE:
THE
CINEMAGRAPH

Depth of field

Depth of field describes the degree to which objects placed at different distances from the lens appear to be in focus. A large depth of field means that objects close to and far from the lens seem to be in sharp focus. Conversely, shallow depth of field describes an image in which objects appear in focus only if they occupy a narrow zone surrounding a single distance in front of the lens. Depth of field is an attribute of the path the light takes through the camera. The focal length of the lens and the camera aperture can be adjusted to change the depth of field for creative effect.

Position

The position of the camera determines the viewpoint of the captured image. A *tripod* is a crucial peripheral device to ensure that, once a vantage point is selected, the camera can be supported.

When a moving image is recorded, the position of the camera may change— this is constrained by the physical attributes of the camera and the surrounding environment.

The camera is a delicate and often expensive instrument, and must be positioned and moved steadily and cautiously, avoiding obstacles, so that it can be operated by one or more people. Hence, demanding a camera position that is moving or more than 5 feet off the ground can be a complicated undertaking.

1.4–1.5 Depth of field
The two performers are the same distance apart in both 1.4 and 1.5, but by adjusting the camera aperture, it is possible to reduce the depth of field and to focus selectively on the foreground or background subject. Even in the virtual domain of CGI, these optical effects are possible, allowing us to direct attention within the **frame**, or simply to emulate real-world cameras.

1.4

1.5

VIDEO IMAGE FORMATS

The most visible characteristic of a video recording is the physical medium on which it is recorded. This may be a digital videotape the size of a paperback book or the size of a matchbox. More and more frequently, however, video is recorded onto high-capacity cards the size of a fingernail, prior to transfer to computer hard drives.

Although the storage options are few, there is considerable variety to the way in which the video information is actually stored on these media devices.

This is because unprocessed, uncompressed video is *enormous*. Information about thousands of **pixels** for many thousands of frames is so voluminous that cost-effective storage and transmission of digital video relies on sophisticated methods of compressing this data. These methods are continuously being refined and improved by manufacturers of imaging hardware and software, with new innovations accompanying successive generations of camcorders. Many of these innovations have evolved from a variety of international analog video formats, inheriting some of the idiosyncrasies of their predecessors.

As a result, the legacy of formats, compression methods, and other parameters that describe how a video frame is captured, recorded, or transmitted can be confusing.

Frame-rate

Frame-rate describes the number of individual frames generated for each second of video. In most of Europe, TV and video systems are comprised of 25 frames per second (fps). In North America, the standard frame-rate for TV and video is 23.976 fps; this is often adjusted to match the standard rate for traditional 35mm film, which is 24 fps. Web-based animations can have custom frame-rates depending on the content; apps and browsers can happily display moving images of varied frame-rates, whereas broadcast and hardware-based systems such as DVD players cannot.

Resolution

The amount of detail in each frame is determined by (a) the size of the video image and (b) the quantity of pixels in each frame. When we consider both values together, we can express the degree of fine detail in an image as **resolution**.

The number of pixels in a video image is usually expressed as the number of pixel-lines, for example, 720 or 1080. The resolution, which considers the pixel dimensions in relation to the physical dimensions of the screen, is expressed in pixels per inch (ppi).

1.6 Storage media
The outward appearance of digital storage media is not a reliable indication of the various parameters that define how the video material is encoded upon it. These parameters are defined by the settings within the recording, playback, or editing hardware or software.

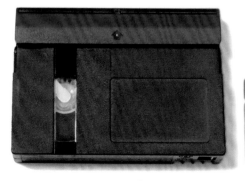

1.6

THE
CAMERA

**VIDEO IMAGE
FORMATS**

VIDEO
COMPRESSION
AND CODECS

STILL IMAGE
FORMATS

SOFTWARE

IMAGE
CREATION

IMAGE
MANIPULATION

TRADITIONAL
ART
MATERIALS

ALTERNATIVE
TOOLS

CASE STUDY:
MOMOCO

EXERCISE:
THE
CINEMAGRAPH

Aspect ratio

The height-to-width relationship of the frame can be expressed as a proportion. For digital video this is typically a 16:9 ratio, but other ratios are used in film or legacy video formats. The **aspect ratio** of traditional 35mm film is 3:2; Apple's iPad currently records video in 4:3, which was for many years the standard for TV and video.

Interlacing options

The lines of pixels may scan or "build" a frame of video one of two ways: either in a *progressive* delivery of first line, then second, then third, etc.; or in an *interlaced* pattern, beginning with the odd-numbered lines (1, 3, 5, etc.) before returning to the top of the frame and filling in the even-numbered lines (2, 4, 6, etc.). An interlaced frame is therefore an interwoven combination of two constituent images called the odd and even "fields."

Of the two methods, progressive scanning is most similar to the frame-by-frame principle of exposing celluloid film one frame at a time; by contrast, interlace scanning requires two cycles of exposure to generate a full frame. Some filmmakers therefore prefer the progressive scanning approach, as the resulting video can appear more "filmic." However, most modern TV and video systems have evolved around interlacing methods: the underlying technologies, platform, and distribution media often dictate the scanning method. Choices about interlacing must be based on a consideration of the full production workflow, rather than aesthetic preferences.

Codec, format

A **codec** is a set of instructions that dictates how a large piece of data (such as video and audio) should be compressed and subsequently decompressed. Commonly encountered video codecs are **H.264**, DV, and **MPEG**.

The format of a file is not the same thing as the codec. The format is a digital container (sometimes called a "wrapper") for associated video and audio files that have already been compressed by various codecs. The format may also contain **metadata**—information about the video and audio and the compression parameters used by the codecs. The format is used by playback software to identify what the media components are and how they can be interpreted. MOV, AVI, and AVCHD are all types of video formats.

VIDEO COMPRESSION AND CODECS

Although image resolution, frame-rate, and interlace options will impact the quality of the recorded video, these have a relatively fixed and predictable impact upon the fidelity of the image. Codecs, however, are infinitely variable and can potentially degrade the image quite drastically. This is because video codecs are principally *lossy* to some extent; that is, they irretrievably remove data that is deemed unnecessary for the video to be more-or-less faithfully reconstituted.

There are two distinct categories of lossy compression method in relation to video: codecs that use *intra*-frame compression only, and those that use *inter*-frame compression as well.

Intra-frame compression removes visual redundancy from a single frame using **JPEG**-like compression; in other words, there is no comparison of adjacent frames, only of adjacent pixels to identify repetition or similarity that could yield more efficient methods of expressing essentially the same data. By contrast, intra-frame compression makes comparisons *between* frames to see if there is any redundancy that can be removed. Hence, if a pixel is blue in frame one, and still blue in the following thousand frames, then this information needs to be stored only once, not a thousand and one times.

Intermediate codecs

Although the preceding codecs provide very efficient means of compressing video data in order to record it to, and play it back from tape or card, the codecs are not terribly friendly when it comes to editing. In order for a device to reconstitute a frame of video in order to display it, the device may have to summon data from earlier or later frames: this is the principle behind inter-frame compression. However, nonlinear editing (NLE) systems will naturally reorder or disrupt the relationships of neighboring frames as we trim clips and place edit points. Thus, the NLE must process and interpret data much more intensively than a camcorder and, at times, playback performance can be affected by this processing load.

To minimize the processing load, some NLEs opt to convert the compressed video into a format that is more amenable to being chopped up and rearranged.

These codecs (called intermediate codecs) typically use intra-frame compression only, so that each individual frame can be built for display without reference to neighboring frames.

A common example of an intermediate codec is Apple's ProRes codec, which is designed for use within the post-production environment only. Once fully edited, video sequences would be transcoded (converted) back to a format that is more suitable for linear playback or transmission.

As a result of this conversion process, a file that occupies only a few gigabytes of storage when recorded onto an SD card may take up far more space once transcoded into the intermediate codec on the NLE. However, the processing load on the NLE is reduced, allowing for smoother playback and for more demanding real-time operations such as **compositing**.

THE
CAMERA

VIDEO IMAGE
FORMATS

VIDEO
COMPRESSION
AND CODECS

STILL IMAGE
FORMATS

SOFTWARE

IMAGE
CREATION

IMAGE
MANIPULATION

TRADITIONAL
ART
MATERIALS

ALTERNATIVE
TOOLS

CASE STUDY:
MOMOCO

EXERCISE:
THE
CINEMAGRAPH

Compression artifacts

Compression is a double-edge sword. Whereas it allows us to store and deliver video sequences more feasibly, data compression leads to compression artifacts: portions of the image where image loss is apparent. These artifacts may not be too detrimental to the viewing experience, but they obstruct the post-production process. For example, in **chroma**-keying (the selective replacement of colored parts of the video image), the boundary between the foreground subject and the colored background (typically green or blue) must be delicately differentiated.

This differentiation can sometimes be undermined by compression artifacts, so care must be taken to preserve the maximum image quality during certain stages of the production workflow, with a corresponding consideration of costs.

The "flavor" of video that you are working with must be carefully assessed, specified, and respected from start to finish to avoid incompatibilities, as well as cost and quality complications.

How a video sequence is compressed

1. Two frames are selected, a fraction of a second apart. The full frame data from these frames (called "**key-frames**") is recorded.

2. By comparing the key-frames, the encoding device predicts what the "in-between" frames should look like.

3. The encoding device now checks to see how accurate its predictions were by comparing the predicted data against the actual data present in those in-between frames.

4. This produces a new data stream called "difference" data: a record of the marginal difference between the true information and the predicted information. This difference data is smaller than the original frame data, so this is stored as a more compact substitute.

5. As long as the decoding device is using the same prediction methods, then it too can work out how to reconstitute the full video sequence based on the key-frame data and the difference data alone. These prediction patterns are governed by consistent mathematical computations that are embedded in the "rules" of each codec.

6. Multiple key-frames are selected throughout the video sequence.

TIP | A SHARED LANGUAGE OF PREDICTED ENCODING

Modern video recording technologies use codecs to store the minimum required information needed for video to be played back. With reference to only a few significant frames of video (key-frames), the codecs can predict what the remaining frames will look like. The codec then compares its prediction with the true frame content. If there is little difference, then only the minimal difference is stored or transmitted. Playback equipment possesses the same intelligent awareness of codecs, so it will only need to be informed of the differences between the predicted frame and the true frame.

STILL IMAGE FORMATS

When light strikes the sensor in a camera, the light and color values are converted from light to three digital signals corresponding to the red, green, and blue primary colors. These signals represent the raw sensor data. However, because the sensor in a camera may have sensitivity to tone or color that exceeds the expressive capabilities of common file formats or display technologies, some processing of the sensor data is required in order to conform the image to a file format that could be interpreted (and therefore displayed or edited) by another device.

Some editing applications, such as Adobe Photoshop, will recognize RAW images and allow you to preview and tweak some of the processing parameters before the file is conformed to a standardized image file format. RAW files are the most faithful record of the recorded image, but they are very large. The standardized file formats will record less of the captured data, but can also reduce the file size further by compressing the data as a *lossless* or a *lossy* image file.

Lossless compression formats

As we know, the information that corresponds to the raster of pixels is actually a series of numerical values. In sequence, these individual pixel values become a colossal stream of numbers. But computers are experts at dealing with numbers, and often the extensive image data we create can be rearranged in order to be expressed more efficiently. Image editing and viewing software is capable of "packing" the stream of data into a more optimal sequence.

If the same value (or string of values) is repeated multiple times in a data stream, it may be more efficient to note the extent of the repetition, rather than record each repetition of the same or similar value. A familiar example is the widespread use of terms such as "btw" to represent the longer phrase "by the way." This is the principle of lossless compression. The compression is achieved by recognizing repetitive patterns and using more concise values to stand in for these recurring strings of longer values. Both camera and image editing software are familiar with these substitute strings, and can restore the original data from the encoded stream. Although some additional processing time and effort is required in order to reassemble the image from the compressed data stream, the benefit is that the stored or transmitted data is smaller.

TIFF is a frequently used image format for single images because it can reduce the size of a file by these lossless methods (although it also supports lossy compression).

THE
CAMERA

VIDEO IMAGE
FORMATS

VIDEO
COMPRESSION
AND CODECS

**STILL IMAGE
FORMATS**

SOFTWARE

IMAGE
CREATION

IMAGE
MANIPULATION

TRADITIONAL
ART
MATERIALS

ALTERNATIVE
TOOLS

CASE STUDY:
MOMOCO

EXERCISE:
THE
CINEMAGRAPH

Lossy compression formats

More substantial compression can be accomplished if we are willing to lose or change some of the numerical data. Lossy compression works on this principle: "If you can't tell it's been removed, it didn't need to be there."

Experts in human vision and digital imaging have devised file formats that can compress visual data this way. JPEG is one such format that can exploit the limitations of human visual perception by intelligently removing or replacing visual data that would not be noticed anyway. For example, in an image of a black, leafless tree set against a blue sky, there will be some fine "fussy" detail—alternating fragments of blue and black—present in the smallest branches of the tree; detail that is barely

perceptible to the eye. The JPEG format uses a compressor that can recognize (and remove) this redundant fine detail, reducing the amount of information that needs to be recorded. At times, the color information may endure more substantial compression than the brightness information, allowing for even greater reduction of file sizes. As long as the compression does not degrade the image too much, we can tolerate some "selective memory" of the original data to benefit from the space efficiencies that lossy compression provides. This is why most digital cameras save photographic images in this specially designed JPEG format, achieving a widely accepted balance between file size and image quality.

Which format do we use?

TIFF and JPEG are two alternative "delivery" formats that are suited to different output media. TIFF, a high-quality lossless format, is suited to high-resolution output such as print; JPEG, a more compact lossy format, is better suited to electronic delivery such as the web.

In practice, many of the digital images that we ultimately use will be composite images that have undergone a number of transformations and adjustments prior to inclusion in a video sequence. Therefore, it makes sense to preserve the maximum quality image possible throughout the workflow. Our image editing software will have its own **proprietary** file format (e.g., **PSD**) that preserves information about these adjustments as well as the original image data.

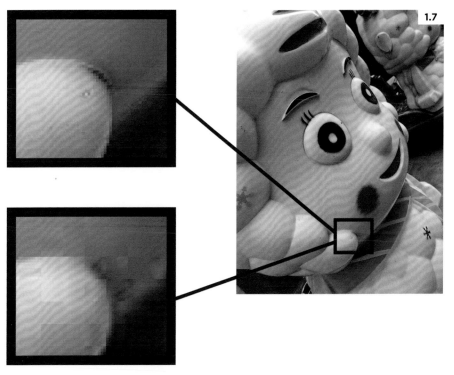

1.7

1.7 Compression artifacts
Digital images can be stored in a variety of file formats. Some formats optimize storage space by permitting the selective loss of data. These lossy formats, such as JPEG, can faithfully store the image data with no perceptible degradation of the image (detail, top). However, if excessive compression is used, blocky artifacts become visible in the image (detail, bottom), and fine detail is sacrificed.

25

SOFTWARE

There are many examples of commercial and free, or shareware, software on the market that are capable of being used for motion graphics. Anything that can be used to create a sequence of images could be used for the production of your source material. You could, for example, produce a sequence of pages in a word processing package and output these as an image sequence, which, when viewed sequentially at speed, produce the illusion of motion. However, for the purpose of this book, we will focus on the most commonly used or commonly available software that is used by practitioners of motion graphics.

As the stated aim is to remain "software agnostic," we will not be recommending any one over another, but will merely explain the purpose of the software and its relative merits.

It is useful to divide the software into two categories: image creation and image manipulation. Image creation is about the acquisition of original material, whether it is created by the user directly (e.g., painting and drawing) or is designed by the user but generated by the computer (e.g., 3D-rendered imagery). Image manipulation concerns things done to the images once they are in the computer. This usually means altering an image or combining multiple images to create a new image, a technique called *compositing*. Many of the software examples can happily fit into either category, but we have classified them by their primary function.

What should I learn?

Although all of these programs have unique interfaces and their own particular methods of workflow, the underlying principles of animation, compositing, modeling, lighting, and camera movement are fundamentally the same across them all. As such, the best option is to learn the one that you have access to through your school or place of work. If you are considering this independently, then most of these programs are offered through a 30-day trial to enable you to try them out. The simplest method is to go and see what feels most comfortable.

Links to relevant software are available on the website at www.bloomsbury.com /crook-motion-graphics.

THE CAMERA

VIDEO IMAGE FORMATS

VIDEO COMPRESSION AND CODECS

STILL IMAGE FORMATS

SOFTWARE

IMAGE CREATION

IMAGE MANIPULATION

TRADITIONAL ART MATERIALS

ALTERNATIVE TOOLS

CASE STUDY: MOMOCO

EXERCISE: THE CINEMAGRAPH

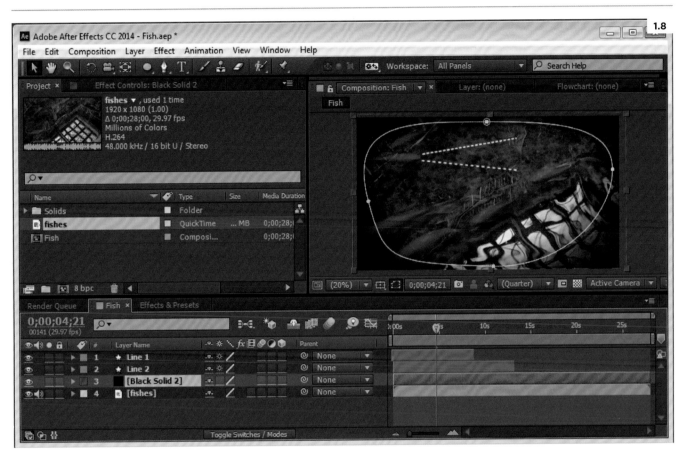

1.8

1.8 Adobe After Effects
After Effects (AE), made by Adobe, is a standard compositing software package that is easy to learn. As a result of its large user base there are numerous books and web-based tutorials available along with many forums offering help, advice, and tips.

IMAGE CREATION

Animation

Software applications for image creation are mostly painting and drawing programs with the addition of a time-based function; that is, the ability to create and alter content over time to give the illusion of motion. Images created are often either **raster** based (i.e., using pixel information) or **vector** based (i.e., generated mathematically using nodes and lines). We have divided image creation into two areas: animation and CGI modeling.

In this section we will focus on software that is used primarily to create two-dimensional (2D) animation. The examples here all take graphic objects and move them around the screen. Most of them automatically move the objects along a path in a process known as **tweening**, meaning that the animation is calculated by the software. Many also offer **onion skinning**, which allows frames before or after the one you are working on to be visible. Both processes tend to produce a flat, cut-out style.

Adobe's Flash was originally developed as an animation tool but later evolved, through its scripting environment, into an industry-standard interactive multimedia program. More recently, through the development of HTML and CSS and because of difficulties viewing Flash files on Apple devices, it has slipped in favor a little. It is still, however, an excellent tool for producing animations. It uses multilayered vector elements to produce tweened and key-framed motion.

ToonBoom Studio and Harmony are two alternatives that work in similar ways to Flash in that they too work with multilayered, vector-based graphics. They have a full bone-rigging tool for character puppetry, and they use timing sheets, like traditional animation. Harmony in particular is becoming an industry standard for 2D animation companies.

CelAction 2D by CelAction is another similar animation tool that uses vector and **raster imagery** on multiple layers with bone rigging and camera moves. It was developed in conjunction with animators Neville Astley and Mark Baker of *Peppa Pig* fame.

A similar, cost-effective product is Anime Studio. This has the addition of "smart bones," a tool that enables the creation of "dials" to control the animation of certain objects on screen; this gives the animator greater flexibility in how they control their elements.

THE
CAMERA

VIDEO IMAGE
FORMATS

VIDEO
COMPRESSION
AND CODECS

STILL IMAGE
FORMATS

SOFTWARE

IMAGE
CREATION

IMAGE
MANIPULATION

TRADITIONAL
ART
MATERIALS

ALTERNATIVE
TOOLS

CASE STUDY:
MOMOCO

EXERCISE:
THE
CINEMAGRAPH

CGI modeling

Pencil is a free downloadable animation program created by Pascal Naidon and Patrick Corrieri. It is a simple animation program that allows hand-drawn animation in both raster and vector formats. It does not allow for tweening but does have onion skinning.

A simpler alternative for those who are not so adept at drawing on the computer is PowToon by PowToon Studios. This is an online piece of software, in that there is nothing to download. It uses a drag-and-drop system with prebuilt actions that, when mixed together, enable the user to develop some complex motions. It has built-in images and sounds but will allow you to import your own and will support the import of Adobe Flash files.

Not normally considered an animation tool, but one that many people have access to, Microsoft PowerPoint can be used to create 2D animation. Through careful use of slide transitions and animation of screen elements, convincing motion graphics can be created quite quickly and easily.

This is software capable of producing 3D-rendered animation. There are many commercial software packages available but, in general, all use detailed models sculpted within the software combined with virtual lights and cameras to produce highly complex and often very realistic motion imagery. They often have a system of incorporating bones into a model to allow for complex jointed animations, known as *inverse kinematics*.

Two of the most popular software packages are 3D Studio Max (3ds Max) and Maya, both made by Autodesk. Both work in similar ways and opinion is split as to the merits of either, with Maya often being favored by visual effects and animation studios and 3D Studio Max by game development and architectural studios. Both have extremely sophisticated lighting, modeling, and rendering engines and can produce photorealistic images.

An alternative is Maxon's Cinema 4D (C4D), which has widespread popularity in schools due to its relatively simple learning curve. It also has similar modeling and **rendering** capabilities, but has a smaller user base, resulting in slightly fewer online tutorials and support forums.

Another alternative is NewTek's Lightwave. This is generally considered to be a high-end program and is often used in the production of feature films. As a result, it is often outside the beginner's reach.

An accessible and freely downloadable alternative is Blender from The Blender Foundation. This is an **open source**, fully featured modeling and animation program that has a large user base with multiple sources of help and support. There is an active Blender community regularly developing new content and ensuring that new features are regularly incorporated.

IMAGE MANIPULATION

Image manipulation is the ability to take existing images and in some way alter them. This may mean distorting the underlying pixel data in order to change or warp an image. More importantly, it allows for the layering of multiple elements (e.g., video, stills, text) on top of each other to produce new results. The way each layer interacts with the layers below affects the visual result.

The grandfather of static image compositing software is Adobe Photoshop. A byword for photo manipulation, Photoshop has extremely powerful editing tools, enabling the user to mask and blend and edit layers in almost limitless ways. Since Photoshop CS6, the **timeline** panel has enabled motion to be created directly within the software; however, earlier versions can still be used to create a series of still images that can be animated in other programs.

A credible free alternative is **GIMP**. It is much the same as Photoshop with many features replicated and, with the addition of the GIMP Animation Plugin (GAP), it is also capable of outputting animated images.

Adobe's flagship motion graphics program, however, is **After Effects**. This, in essence, is Photoshop for the moving image. It enables static and motion elements to be seamlessly composited over multiple layers and across time. There are numerous effects that can be employed with multiple adjustable parameters. There are also numerous built-in generators for creating particle effects. What makes this so powerful is that almost every parameter can be adjusted over time, which results in endless possibilities and configurations.

The Apple equivalent is Motion. This also enables the compositing and blending of layers over time with many built-in effects and particle generators. The general consensus, however, is that Motion has an easier learning curve, but After Effects is capable of better results.

There are a number of commercially available nonlinear editors (NLEs) that can also be considered motion graphic tools. Two of the most accessible are Adobe Premiere and Apple Final Cut. Whereas these are not specifically designed as motion graphic tools, they are capable of a large number of compositing effects in that elements can be blended together and key-framed over time.

At the high end of compositing there is The Foundry's **Nuke**. This is used on many large-scale film and TV productions for compositing visual effects shots. This is not layer-based like many of the previously mentioned examples, but instead it uses a **node-based** system to add effects. Effects are added to a flowchart building up a complex composite in the process. The ability to quickly "rewire" nodes to alter the effect is extremely powerful.

Another credible alternative is Natron, a freely downloadable open-source, node-based compositor that has an interface very similar to Nuke's. Natron is designed to make it easy to learn.

1.9 Natron

Natron is a node-based compositor. It is very similar in look and feel to Nuke. It is open source and capable of using open FX plugins, meaning that it is highly expandable.

It is available free of charge from https://natron.inria.fr

Smoke image: Francois "Coyhot" Grassard

Catwalk image: Alessandro Dalla Fontana

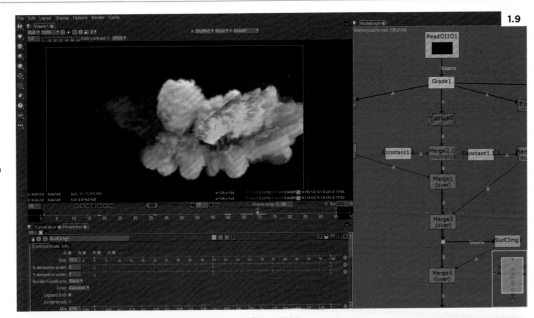

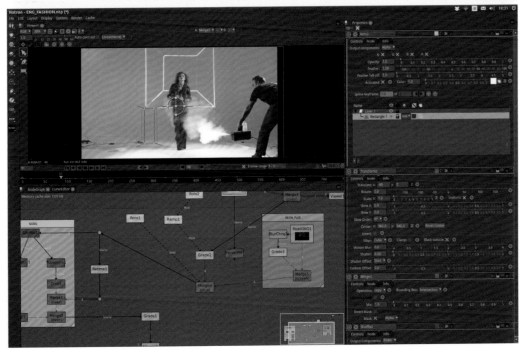

TRADITIONAL ART MATERIALS

Pen and pencil

When thinking of producing motion graphics it is very easy to dive straight for the computer. The impulse to fire up whatever software you favor using and begin the art of creating is great; however, it is worth pausing before you begin. There is a rich vein of media available to you that has existed for centuries before computers were even considered. Traditional art materials should be part of your toolkit, regardless of your perceived artistic ability. Whether these are used as part of the design and planning process before you begin or are an integral part of the finished work, there is no motion graphic that cannot benefit from their use. By exploring the effects these materials are capable of producing, you will find a visual aesthetic that offers much more than the potentially sterile environment of the computer alone.

Increasingly, pens and pencils are falling out of everyday favor to be replaced by electronic means of mark-making. Visually, this is a shame. A computer reproduces a line or a mark with no variation. Each line is a clone of the one before it. With pens and pencils each mark has its own character and no two will be exactly the same. This will give your marks dynamism and life even before they have any motion applied to them.

Pencils come in many different degrees of hardness, from 9H (H standing for *hard*) to 9B (B standing for *black*) with the midpoint being represented by F (standing for *fine*). The most commonly found pencil hardness is HB (*hard black*), which is considered the best for writing. The farther toward 9H you head, the finer and lighter the line produced will be. Nearer to 9B, the softer and blacker the line will be. 2B pencils onward have the ability to be smudged, producing soft, shaded edges. H pencils onward will not really smudge but can be used for fine detail. Along with hardness, it should be remembered that pencils also come in a wide variety of colors, which, when blended, produce an infinite variety of shades.

Pens also come in a huge variety of colors and delivery mechanisms. Ballpoints are possibly the most widely available, producing a line of fairly even thickness, but with some variation of tone depending on the surface and pressure being used. Fiber tips produce a denser line and are less susceptible to pressure variation. Fountain, reservoir, or dip pens produce the widest variety of lines due to the way the ink is transferred from the nib. The nature of these pens to blot or splatter can produce a really pleasing aesthetic.

THE
CAMERA

VIDEO IMAGE
FORMATS

VIDEO
COMPRESSION
AND CODECS

STILL IMAGE
FORMATS

SOFTWARE

IMAGE
CREATION

IMAGE
MANIPULATION

TRADITIONAL
ART
MATERIALS

ALTERNATIVE
TOOLS

CASE STUDY:
MOMOCO

EXERCISE:
THE
CINEMAGRAPH

Charcoal, chalk, and pastel

Charcoal is the oldest-known art material. Burnt sticks were used to make marks on cave walls by our earliest ancestors. Charcoal now is usually made from burnt willow. It produces a rich, dark black and can easily be blended to produce subtle gradations of tone. It can also be used to produce fine lines. It is, however, quite messy to work with and work can easily be accidentally smudged. To solve this problem, the image needs to be "fixed" by spraying it with a fine layer of fixative. Hairspray is a reasonable, cheap alternative.

Chalk is one of a number of natural minerals, commonly red, black, or white, that is shaped into drawing implements. Like charcoal, it can be used tonally or linearly, and if wetted before use produce a richer color.

Most of what we think of as chalk nowadays is artificial chalk, whereby pigment is ground up and mixed with a binding medium to produce a paste, giving us the term *pastel*. Pastels come in two varieties: the powdery chalk type and the ones bound with an oil (known as *oil pastels*). These are more like crayons and produce extremely bright and vibrant colors.

Paper

There are likely as many varieties of paper surface as there are materials to put on them. *Papers* come in different thicknesses and a variety of textures and finishes. It can be coated or not, glossy or matte. It can be textured (like watercolor paper) or smooth (like cartridge paper). Handmade paper is often highly textured and may have other materials embedded into it.

From the point of view of motion graphics, paper can supply an organic texture over which other elements can be layered.

Clay

Traditionally used as a sculpting material, *clay* should not be discounted as a material to use in motion graphics. In its wet state it is highly malleable and can be manipulated into many different shapes.

More commonly used is polymer modeling clay, which does not set. *Polymer clay* has the advantage of coming in a large variety of colors and being easily manipulated. Aardman Animations is one of the world's experts in working in clay.

1.10 Chalkboard animation
Chalk on a blackboard is an easy material to work with and something that most people have experience doing.

It also has a connotation of schools and education, so if your motion graphic is an educational piece this may be an entirely suitable option.

1.10

Paint and ink

Paint is a solid-colored pigment bound up in a liquid medium. It is traditionally transferred to a surface with a brush and is often diluted with another medium, such as water or oil. There are many different variations of paint and each has its own possibilities in the production of motion graphics.

Watercolor paints can be liquid in a tube or solid in a block, but both, as the name suggests, are diluted with water to produce translucent colors that can be layered over each other. The watery nature of the paint can be used to great effect. Normally they are used on watercolor paper, although any thick paper will work.

Oil paints are bound in oil and usually diluted with a mixture of turpentine and linseed oil. They produce a much richer, opaque surface, and can be applied thickly to produce surface texture. As a result of the use of oil they tend to take a long time to dry, but to the motionographer this could be an advantage, because the paint can be manipulated before drying. Oils are usually used on stretched canvas or boards. They need a stiff, nonabsorbent surface.

Gouache is similar to watercolor except the pigment contains an amount of white that tends to produce more vibrant and opaque colors. Cheap versions of gouache are sometimes referred to as *poster paint* and is often the kind of paint used in schools.

Acrylics are bound up in acrylic medium and as a result can be painted onto many different surfaces. Household emulsion is a kind of acrylic. Acrylics also produce an opaque color and can be worked like oils and gouache.

Inks used for drawing and design tend to be known as *India ink*. They can be waterproof and water soluble. Waterproof inks produce the richest colors and can be copied easily. Water-soluble inks behave more like watercolors and can be diluted for translucency. Adding waterproof inks to water can also produce some interesting results and is the fundamental technique used in marbling.

Photography

Although some may argue that *photography* is not a traditional art, it is most certainly an important tool in the production of motion graphics. Stills can be used as graphical elements in themselves and provide hue and texture to a composition. They can also be used as an image sequence, the individual images being re-photographed to produce a new motion sequence.

It is important to note that an expensive camera is not always necessary. Some excellent results can be achieved using the camera in your phone.

THE
CAMERA

VIDEO IMAGE
FORMATS

VIDEO
COMPRESSION
AND CODECS

STILL IMAGE
FORMATS

SOFTWARE

IMAGE
CREATION

IMAGE
MANIPULATION

TRADITIONAL
ART
MATERIALS

ALTERNATIVE
TOOLS

CASE STUDY:
MOMOCO

EXERCISE:
THE
CINEMAGRAPH

1.11 Watercolor motion
This example from Meg Soro is a student project explaining a journey along the Appalachian Trail. It beautifully combines camera moves and rotoscoping with the natural action of watercolors. The paint not only provides color and texture, but also drives the motion along the trail.

www.megsoro.com

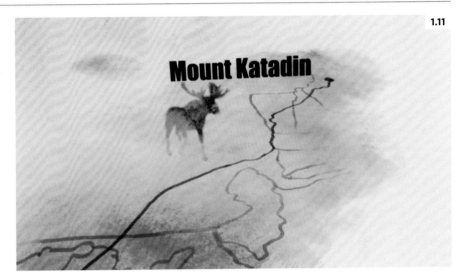

1.11

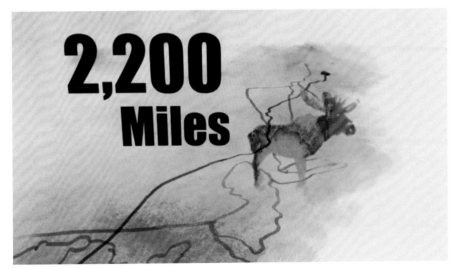

ALTERNATIVE TOOLS

We have looked at the software available in the production of motion graphics and have seen that it is easy to think no further than this. We have also seen that there is a plethora of art materials that we can use to add life and character to our work. If this was as far as we went it would be possible to produce some fantastic examples of motion graphics. However, if we open our eyes and look at the world around us, we see that there are an infinite number of resources that we could use as the basis or inspiration for our motion graphics. Combine these alternative tools with the ideas we have just described and the possibility of producing something truly unique is highly likely.

Stop-motion

Many of the examples we discuss here are given life through the use of **stop-motion** (see page 110). Fundamentally, stop-motion is the technique of moving an inanimate object a small amount between shots, so when these shots are viewed sequentially it gives the illusion of motion. Anything can be animated in this method.

Toys and household objects

Toys make exceptionally good objects for motion graphics. Many already have moveable parts that can be used to bring the object to life. Dolls and action figures are simple but ready-made **armature** puppets. Vehicles can be brought to life. Games can be made to play themselves.

There is a large community dedicated to making animation and motion graphics using building blocks such as LEGO®. The huge success of *The LEGO® Movie* is testament to this (although it should be noted that in that case it was CGI, made to look like stop-motion LEGO®). However, using the blocks to build objects and then animating these to simulate a realistic scene is only one way. An alternative is to consider the colored blocks as pixels in a low-resolution image and then building the images frame by frame. An early example of this technique would be the work of Michel Gondry and his video for The White Stripes' song "Fell in Love with a Girl."

Household objects should also be considered. Study an object, a corkscrew for example, and think about what its intrinsic action is. Then think about how stop-motion could be used to bring life to the inanimate object. Think about what the properties of the material are. Clear hair gel could be used as water, shaving foam could be used as steam. Animators such as The Brothers Quay and Jan Svankmeyer were masters of this technique as early as the 1970s.

THE
CAMERA

VIDEO IMAGE
FORMATS

VIDEO
COMPRESSION
AND CODECS

STILL IMAGE
FORMATS

SOFTWARE

IMAGE
CREATION

IMAGE
MANIPULATION

TRADITIONAL
ART
MATERIALS

**ALTERNATIVE
TOOLS**

CASE STUDY:
MOMOCO

EXERCISE:
THE
CINEMAGRAPH

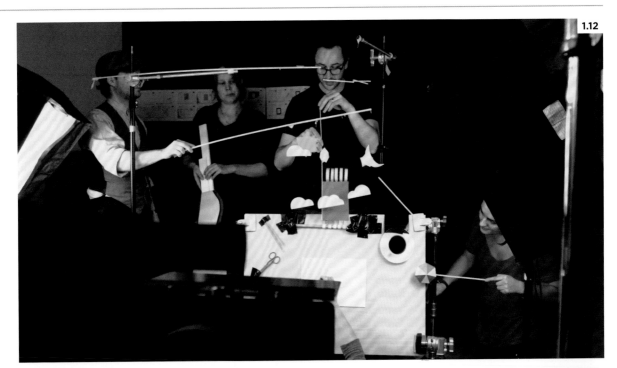

1.12

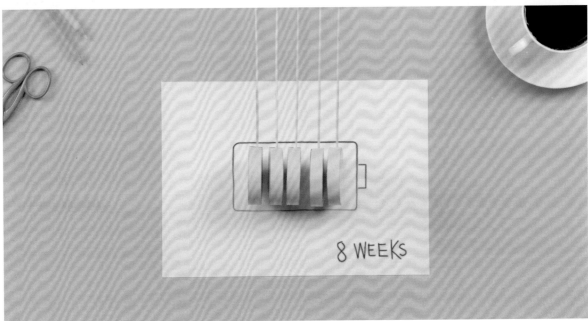

1.12 Kindle White production
Behind the scenes of the Kindle White
commercial, in which we can see the team making
use of studio-made props to simulate the digital
processes of the eReader.

People

If you don't have access to objects to use in your motion graphics, there is always the possibility to use yourself. The process of using people as stop-motion puppets is known as "pixilation," a technique devised by Norman McLaren, and the term was coined at the National Film Board of Canada by McLaren and Grant Munro. Pixilation requires a person to be photographed in sequence, moving slightly between each shot, giving the illusion of movement. To really make this effective and to counter the argument of "why not just film the person?" the person should move in ways that would not be possible naturally. By moving a step at a time but standing up in each shot, the figure can be made to glide across the floor. If each shot is taken when the subject is jumping, the person can be made to hover in midair. The more fantastic the motion, the more effective the technique.

Technology

Rather than creating all of the material for your motion graphic yourself, it is possible to use Internet technology to crowdsource your material. *Crowdsourcing* is the process of asking members of the public to submit material to you that you can then compile into a finished piece. An excellent example of this is Airbnb's "Hollywood & Vines," where, using social media, shot requests were tweeted out for members of the public to film using the Vine app and were then compiled into a complete film.

The organization required to successfully complete a truly crowdsourced piece is great; however the process could also be achieved by an individual by making use of numerous video and photo-sharing sites. These can be scoured for suitable material that is then compiled into one piece. The real danger with this, however, is copyright permission. If you use an element created by someone else, you need to ensure that you have the owner's permission to use it. Look for elements that display the **Creative Commons** logo and then check their usage license.

Other possible resources include Google Earth and Google Street View. These give highly detailed images of locations that can then be re-photographed, moving the location between images to give the illusion of driving down a street or flying over a landscape. As above, **copyright clearance** must be obtained if you are going to use the material externally.

THE
CAMERA

VIDEO IMAGE
FORMATS

VIDEO
COMPRESSION
AND CODECS

STILL IMAGE
FORMATS

SOFTWARE

IMAGE
CREATION

IMAGE
MANIPULATION

TRADITIONAL
ART
MATERIALS

**ALTERNATIVE
TOOLS**

CASE STUDY:
MOMOCO

EXERCISE:
THE
CINEMAGRAPH

Replacements

Another technique related to stop-motion uses replacements. These are a sequence of elements, either two-dimensional images or three-dimensional models, that when re-photographed produce the illusion of motion. An example might be to take a series of still photographs of a person walking. Each photo is then printed onto a separate sheet. Each sheet is then photographed in another location in sequence, moving each sheet slightly forward of the previous one. When viewed as a movie, the effect is that the person is now walking in a new location.

Similar effects can be achieved by creating a series of physical objects that change sequentially over time. When these objects are re-photographed in a new situation, they give the illusion of movement. The advantage of this method is that, being three dimensional, the objects can be photographed from multiple angles, giving a wider variety of shots.

The natural world

The natural world should also be considered as a source of motion graphic material. Through the use of time-lapse photography, whereby a camera takes a series of stills over a set period of time, the natural motion of elements that may normally be considered static are revealed. Relatively fast movement such as clouds can seem to flow like liquid, while slow movements such as plant growth become highly dynamic.

Putting it together

These individual techniques, in isolation, are not necessarily motion graphics. They are, however, valuable elements that, when combined with others, can provide your motion graphic project with something unique. What you use, and how, are really only limited by your imagination.

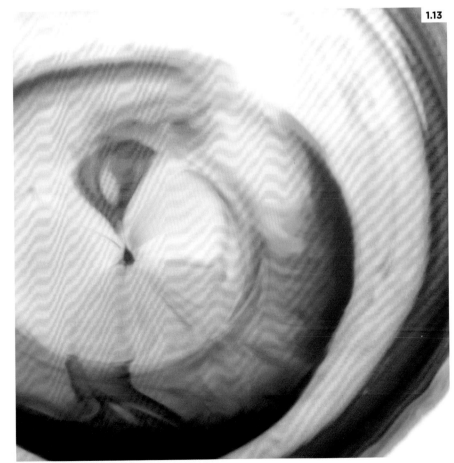

1.13

1.13 A milk kaleidoscope
An interesting effect can be achieved with a shallow dish or saucer of milk. Add a few drops of food coloring onto the surface. Different colors work well. Focus your camera onto the surface, and then add one drop of dish soap into the center of each color. The liquid reacts with the surface tension of the milk, dragging the food coloring into a moving kaleidoscope of mixing colors.

Please see www.bloomsbury.com/crook-motion-graphics for more on this project.

CASE STUDY:
MOMOCO

Momoco is an Emmy award-winning and BAFTA-nominated creative studio. The firm has produced film design, branding, commercials, and animation for 14 years. Well known worldwide for its main title sequences, Momoco has collaborated with directors such as Richard Curtis, Ridley Scott, Lasse Halström, Kevin Spacey, and Dustin Hoffman. The team is led by Creative Director Nic Benns with Design Director Miki Kato, who together answer questions about working on title sequences.

Can you talk us through the production process of one of your title sequences?

On *Fortitude*, we pitched several concepts—one was a sequence where we follow a blood trail that forms shapes under the snow—mammoth bones . . . fingers . . . a pick axe. At the end we find the trails have drawn the town. Another direction was a macro-micro journey—a body dying in the ice and becoming the environment. Ice crystals evolve into aerial views of rivers. These flow into the victim's beard. We fly over trees, the branches become the victim's brain freezing over, etc. The winning board showed that snowflakes can be beautiful but they're also scary close up—like blades and spines.

We contacted time-lapse photographers, Oxford Scientific films, and people experienced in shooting crystals. We even planned to set up in an ice bar in London. After shooting various tests with crystals it was evident that we needed more control and the schedule was tight so we ventured into 3D using **particle systems**. I always say that you can't beat nature. I usually shoot organic elements laterally, but this was an exception.

The first half of the song [featured in the title sequence] was about how fragile and beautiful nature is while the chorus connoted that when nature turns against us, we're helpless. I sketched out a narrative that reflected the beauty of ice and that it can't be tamed. As the sequence progresses the same crystals become labyrinthine and claustrophobic.

We produced 22 scenes including one with a spider's web being frozen over—"even the hunter is trapped." The producers wanted the sequence simpler so we eventually halved the shots. It's just as haunting and it breathes.

What sort of specifications do you get from the client? How much information do you get?

The first meeting, we listen. Sometimes the director may have the seed of a concept but most often we're free and they're open. In film, we're shown an excerpt to get the feel (it's hard to reference texture and style from a script, especially comedy).

The director or producer may give us a synopsis and the rest is research. TV shows prefer to swamp us with several scripts so we can see the story and character arc. Sometimes they haven't shot an episode yet and need a designer to create the branding, which can evolve into a title sequence down the line. If this is the case, we'll talk with the production designer and ask for mood boards of how the world will look. We then pitch **storyboards** or tests depending on how many producers need to sign off.

What is the key to a successful title sequence?

Strong concept, emotion, solid execution, and giving good *credit* to the artists and technicians that made that film or show. The sequence can be close to pure art but it has to deliver information. A good main title tells a story, sets the tone, and introduces the reality the audience is about to enter. It's ideal to do this in a way where the typography is also organic to that world—interacting.

How important is it to tell a story in that one minute before the program?

Sometimes it's essential to build a background—a prologue to the film if it's not established in the script or has been filtered through editing.

There was one drama, *Father & Son*, where it wasn't clear that the lead character had a criminal past, so I designed the sequence as a prologue exploring the character's history in the form of bleeding microfiche.

There was a version of the *One Day* titles, where we collaborated with the screenwriter David Nicholls to produce a character animation of the two lovers growing up, and how their lives mirrored and entwined before we meet them in the flesh. Some sequences are like a brief, fluid history lesson.

1.14 *Fortitude*
The title sequence made by Momoco for the Arctic-based drama *Fortitude* features a landscape of ice and snow crystals that is on the one hand beautiful to look at but on the other forms a metaphor for being trapped, a perfect analogy for the themes of the program.

1.14

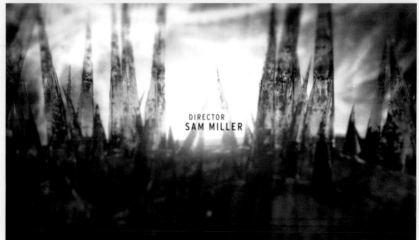

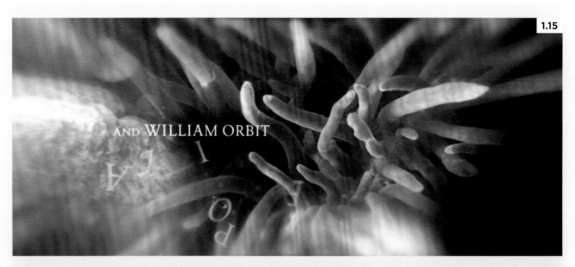

THE
CAMERA

VIDEO IMAGE
FORMATS

VIDEO
COMPRESSION
AND CODECS

STILL IMAGE
FORMATS

SOFTWARE

IMAGE
CREATION

IMAGE
MANIPULATION

TRADITIONAL
ART
MATERIALS

ALTERNATIVE
TOOLS

**CASE STUDY:
MOMOCO**

EXERCISE:
THE
CINEMAGRAPH

What sort of timescale do you generally have to work to?

Three weeks for a TV main title, two months for a film. In TV there are many executive producers that need to approve the development stages, which leaves less time for production. The shortest period we've had for a feature (from briefing to delivery) is a weekend. I remember the call—"what can you deliver in 36 hours?"

What software do you usually use?

The Adobe kit, plus C4D.

What was it that got you interested in working in motion graphics?

Through my teens I wanted to be a comic book artist. I loved the work of John Byrne and Walter Simonson. I drew my own stories for years and was very interested in the relationship between image, type, and sound effects to tell a story. Titles became a more abstract evolution of this.

What training did you do?

The tools are always self-taught. Education comes from trial and error, while studying the editing and structure of feature films. I studied graphic arts at Anglia University, Cambridge (UK), and then was in the film school at CalArts (US), where I met Miki.

What is a typical day at Momoco?

The day starts with the team peeling me off the floor as another all-nighter rolls over. Breakfast meetings in the morning with clients, then the day starts. We're across nine jobs at a time in different stages of production—some are titles, others commercial work. We also have our own personal projects that get edged in where possible. If I'm pitching I'll gather elements from the researcher along with her synopsis of the film so I can start painting up boards. Miki Kato and I create the storyboards. Sometimes we'll have a guest designer work on a pitch if there's a budget.

We animate throughout the day, directing our team too (two or three artists), and then do admin and accounting on Thursdays. The evenings are the best time for design. The nightshift is Jim Fisher—he's been with us eight years. One newspaper said "we're a small studio with big ideas." We keep small. Momoco has a family-like atmosphere.

What project would you work on if given the chance?

Everyone wants to do a Bond title because of its heritage and expectancy as an event. I also like working on horror genre projects (psychological, not visceral).

What advice would you offer to someone starting out in motion graphics?

Concept—the idea—is first. You don't need high-end tools to execute high-end ideas.

Design or film school is an amazing privilege of time. Use it to make mistakes, explore, and research while you don't have the constraints of clients and brand politics. This time can fuel you and develop your voice for many years.

What does motion graphics mean to you?

I've always felt graphic design is *typography*-led and motion graphics is motion design (which I prefer as a term). It's animation but not character driven. The methodology isn't contained—it can be digital or filmed, it can be code or performance.

www.momoco.co.uk

1.15 *THE SHELL*

THE SHELL, also known as *Copelia*, is a 20-minute sci-fi short directed by Nic Benns and produced by Momoco. It tells of a scientific experiment gone wrong where a community is trapped under a human-made organic shell. Both the titles and the actual film rely heavily on CGI and chroma-key visuals with a dark color palette and rich textures, which adds to the claustrophobic atmosphere. For more on chroma-keying, see page 126.

https://vimeo.com/61185726

EXERCISE:
THE CINEMAGRAPH

Summary

A cinemagraph is part way between a photograph and a video. At first glance it appears as a still image, but on further viewing a small portion of the image will have some small, subtle motion. If done well they can be beautiful and highly compelling. The term was coined by fashion photographer Jamie Beck and web designer Kevin Burg in 2011.

The idea is based on a concept introduced in 1989 when CompuServe released version 89a of their **.GIF** file format, adding the functionality to include a sequence or stack of images in one image file with metadata included that describes the speed of reveal of each image. An animated .GIF can play once, loop repeatedly, or "bounce" back and forth between the start frame and the end frame. Normally the whole image changes, just like a film sequence. In this way the first moving images were introduced to the World Wide Web.

A cinemagraph is exactly the same, except that rather than the entire image changing, only a small portion changes. The majority of the image is static and the movement is used to enhance the frozen nature of the scene. In this way, the photograph appears to have captured a small portion of time in a still image.

Requirements

Essential:

- a camera capable of capturing video
- a computer
- video software capable of exporting the video as an image sequence, OR
- image-editing software capable of importing the video as a sequence of images (e.g., Adobe Photoshop or GIMP)

Desirable:

- a tripod

Step 1

You will need to capture some video footage as the basis for your cinemagraph. The type of scene that works best is one where there are defined areas of movement and areas that are static. A busy traffic intersection could work, as there will be constant movement as well as areas that can be held static. A flag fluttering in the breeze would also work well. The motion you are looking for is short (perhaps two seconds) and capable of looping.

A static camera is essential for the illusion to work. Ideally you would place the camera on a tripod; however, you could just as easily wedge the camera into a solid area where it is not likely to move. Be careful of introducing movement when you press the shutter release. If this is likely, shoot more footage than you need, as you will be able to select a small portion of it where, hopefully, the camera is static.

THE
CAMERA

VIDEO IMAGE
FORMATS

VIDEO
COMPRESSION
AND CODECS

STILL IMAGE
FORMATS

SOFTWARE

IMAGE
CREATION

IMAGE
MANIPULATION

TRADITIONAL
ART
MATERIALS

ALTERNATIVE
TOOLS

CASE STUDY:
MOMOCO

**EXERCISE:
THE
CINEMAGRAPH**

Step 2

Once you have recorded the footage, import it into your computer.

Using either an image-editing program or a video-editing program, cut the clip down to the small section you are going to use and then export the footage as an image sequence. At this point you should save the files in an uncompressed format (such as .TIF or .BMP) in order to preserve the quality as much as possible. Make sure that the images are named sequentially (myImage001, myImage002, etc.) in order to help the reincorporation into a sequence.

Step 3

Now import the image sequence back into your image-editing program. It is important that each image or frame of the sequence is imported as a separate layer. You should end up with a stack of images on top of each other.

Step 4

Now the art!

On the first image you need to identify the area that has the movement that you hope to retain. Using whatever selection tool you like (lasso, magic wand, etc.), make a selection around it. You can be as wide as possible to encompass all of the motion, but do not take in any areas of motion that you do not want. Check that the selection is large enough and tight enough on each layer. Feather the selection to give a nice soft edge.

Once you are happy with your selection, invert it so that you are selecting everything else instead.

1.16 Cinemagraph framing
Frame your shot for the cinemagraph so that the area that you want to have moving is separate from the area that you are going to freeze.

1.16

Step 5

On each layer other than the initial one, delete or mask out the area of the selection, leaving *only* the area of movement. This will leave one complete layer and a series of layers where only a small section is visible.

Step 6

Hide all of the layers apart from the initial one. Export the single layer as the first frame of a new sequence (newImage001). Again, ensure at this point you are saving the images in an uncompressed format such as TIFF.

Step 7

Then turn on the next layer in the stack, leaving the initial one visible too. Export this image as the next frame in the sequence (newImage002).

Then turn off the second layer and turn on the third, ensuring that the initial layer is still visible. Export this image in the sequence (newImage003).

Continue until you have saved all of the layers.

1.17 Cinemagraph sequence
Ensure that all of the frames you are using are in a folder together and named sequentially so that they appear in order.

1.17

MAH00265016 MAH00265017 MAH00265018 MAH00265019 MAH00265020 MAH00265021

MAH00265022 MAH00265023 MAH00265024 MAH00265025 MAH00265026 MAH00265027

MAH00265028 MAH00265029 MAH00265030 MAH00265031 MAH00265032 MAH00265033

MAH00265034 MAH00265035 MAH00265036 MAH00265037 MAH00265038 MAH00265039

MAH00265040 MAH00265041 MAH00265042 MAH00265043 MAH00265044 MAH00265045

THE
CAMERA

VIDEO IMAGE
FORMATS

VIDEO
COMPRESSION
AND CODECS

STILL IMAGE
FORMATS

SOFTWARE

IMAGE
CREATION

IMAGE
MANIPULATION

TRADITIONAL
ART
MATERIALS

ALTERNATIVE
TOOLS

CASE STUDY:
MOMOCO

**EXERCISE:
THE
CINEMAGRAPH**

Step 8

In your image-editing program, import the new series of images as an image sequence. You can now save this out again, this time as a .GIF. Make sure the export settings have animation turned on, timing set loop, and the quality set as high as possible (256 colors). If you have the option to set the timings of individual frames, do so, experimenting with the timing.

You should now be able to view your beautiful cinemagraph in a web browser of your choice.

Uses

Think about where and how you might use your cinemagraph. Originally they were used in fashion, but they are often used in advertising and marketing as a means of producing high-quality images with the added ability to draw people's attention. Anywhere a high-quality image is desirable, but a video is too much, a cinemagraph could be a great alternative.

1.18 Cinemagraph masking
Mask out or delete the areas of the image in each frame that you want to have moving so that the area that is going to be frozen is hidden.

Please see www.bloomsbury.com/crook-motion-graphics for more on this project.

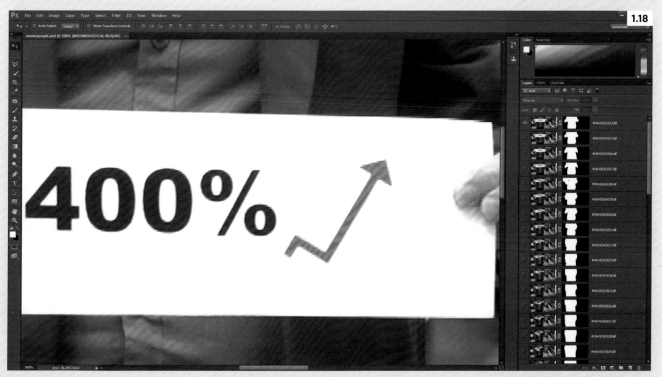

47

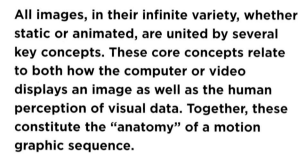

CHAPTER TWO
CONCEPTS:
THE IMAGE

There are infinite possibilities for us to arrange and selectively change various visual elements in order to create dynamic and harmonious motion graphics. Every new composition is unique.

All images, in their infinite variety, whether static or animated, are united by several key concepts. These core concepts relate to both how the computer or video displays an image as well as the human perception of visual data. Together, these constitute the "anatomy" of a motion graphic sequence.

In this chapter, we explore these concepts in order to see under the surface of a motion graphic. This enables us to make more informed decisions about motion graphic design, production, and delivery.

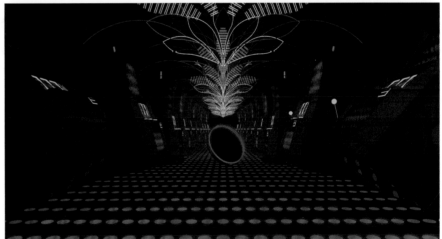

2.1 *Las Vegas*
The literal meaning of "image" is a reflection, or optical counterpart of a real-world thing. But so much of what we experience in motion graphics has no material reality. For this promotional film for William Hill Bookmakers, Bark and Bite constructed a neon Las Vegas boulevard, complete with rolling dice and an incoming jet plane. The images are an illusion; a skilled fabrication of light and color that come to life on the screen.

THE PIXEL

The *pixel* is the smallest component in a digital photographic image and thus a moving image.

The moving image

When we watch a moving image, what is really happening is that a series of still images are being flashed in front of our eyes in sequence at a great speed. We do not distinguish between the separate images (called *frames*) because of a psychological principle called the **persistence of vision**, which means that each separate image resides briefly in our visual memory until the next one arrives. We experience the series of frames as continuous and flowing.

The digital frame

In digital video, each frame is comprised of a "mosaic" of millions of colored "tiles." The miniscule tiles extend horizontally and vertically in columns and rows in a rectangular grid called a *raster*. The tiles of this raster image are called *pixels* (from "*pic*ture *el*ements"), and each pixel possesses its own fixed position and its own variable color value.

The color of an individual pixel is stored as a numerical value that the video display technology can interpret as a specific color. The frame image may depict a variety of textures, tones, and colors, such as the graduated highlights, mid-tones, and shadows that we see in the skin-tones apparent on a face. This apparent graduation is possible because of the subtle variance of similar color values that adjacent pixels possess.

An array of numbers

Whereas we might perceive the image in a frame of video as an arrangement of real-world "objects" (e.g., people, text, environment, explosions), the visual information that is actually stored is a matrix of numerical values that correspond to the pixel tiles.

Whenever we edit, combine, composite, color, or hide a video frame or a portion of the frame, we are instructing the computer to adjust the numbers that represent all or some of the pixels. As we manipulate tangible objects on the timeline of motion graphics software, adjusting their position, transparency, or color, the computer responds accordingly by adjusting the numerical values of each affected pixel, and an altered video image is produced. The pixels' values are continuously updated or recalculated—row by row, frame by frame—into the series of raster images that we perceive as a moving image sequence.

Video is comprised of frames, which are comprised of pixels, which are made of nothing more than numbers—lots and lots of numbers. However we might conceptualize an animated or composited sequence, in truth, motion graphics and video compositing are possible simply because computers are excellent number-crunching machines.

2.2

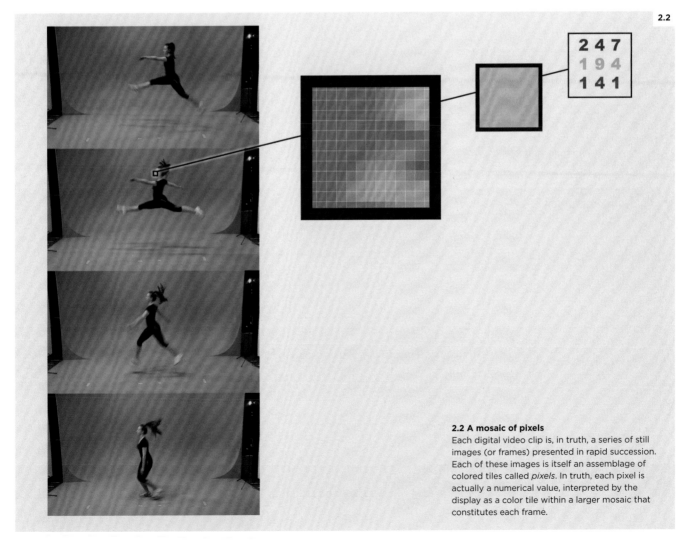

2.2 A mosaic of pixels
Each digital video clip is, in truth, a series of still images (or frames) presented in rapid succession. Each of these images is itself an assemblage of colored tiles called *pixels*. In truth, each pixel is actually a numerical value, interpreted by the display as a color tile within a larger mosaic that constitutes each frame.

DESIGN ELEMENTS

We have seen how each frame of a movie sequence contains a fixed number of picture elements called *pixels*. As far as the computer is concerned, this array of elements is substituted each frame by millions of replacement elements.

By contrast, when we regard a frame of a movie or the movie itself, we do not recognize the image as a dense mosaic of tiny color tiles. As far as we are concerned, we encounter a more modest quantity of tangible objects on an **image plane** or canvas—objects that seemingly possess their own varied height, width, color, and position relative to each other. These objects may be shapes, words, human figures or faces, or other foreground objects that we distinguish as being separate from the textures, colors, or collected objects that constitute a background.

When we create a motion graphic sequence, these are the objects that we place, manipulate, and reposition in time and space. For example, imagine a blue square that slowly migrates over a period of 10 seconds from the bottom center of a white canvas to the top. We are happy for the computer to read this square and background canvas as a sequence of tiny particles if it makes the calculations work, but it is far more intuitive of us to regard this as a single **sprite** making a short journey across the frame.

As well as simple geometric shapes, we may also distinguish figures, faces, words, flames, dollar bills, spaceships, you name it. From a design perspective, it helps to reduce the abundance of potential visual objects into abstract and simplified categories. We call these abstract categories *design elements*. To conceptualize them this way allows us to define some general principles that will guide us as to how elements should be arranged, regardless of specific visual content.

2.3

2.3 Design elements in action
In this film from Tendril, multiple design elements are used together. Shapes, lines, points, and type are combined into a pleasing whole.

www.tendril.ca

Point

The most rudimentary design element is a *point*. A point may have no visible characteristic, and may serve only as a reference coordinate around which other elements may move.

Line

Line connects points. Line possesses length and direction. A line may be straight, curved, or irregular, and may have varying weight. Lines are useful for imposing structure and order, as they can connect, separate, or enclose. They are also useful for providing emphasis; lines can outline or underscore, or lead the eye toward other elements.

Shape

Shapes may be geometric (e.g., circles, squares, triangles) or organic. Some organic shapes may be recognizable in their outline (e.g., figures, animals, buildings) whereas others are easier to classify by analogy (e.g., tear-shaped, egg-shaped, kidney-shaped).

Shapes in repetition may be perceived as unified patterns rather than separate components.

Shapes possess area and color or tone, and in relation to each other may possess mass or weight.

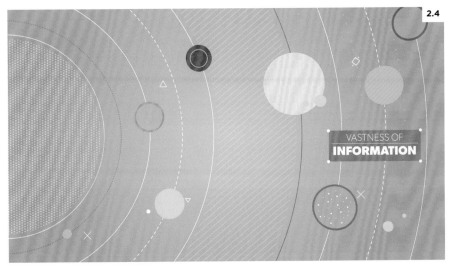

2.4

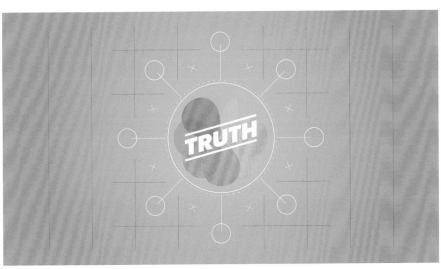

2.4 Lines and shapes
Lines and shapes are used diagrammatically to direct the viewers' attention. The simplicity of the design does not detract from the complex information being portrayed.

Value

All elements have a *value*, which is a tone (e.g., a brightness value), but may also be a color (i.e., a hue). Value can provide texture and direction; the eye can be directed around a canvas by the transition between light and dark. Tone or color can also supply emphasis or delineation to other elements; *drop shadow* or *emboss* filters are commonly used examples.

Type

In truth, *type* is a collection of lines and shapes, but these aggregate into recognizable symbols that possess, in addition to color, weight, and direction, an intrinsic linguistic meaning. Type also bears a sophisticated communicative legacy; a lean, futuristic typeface conveys something very different from an ornate black-letter **font**, even when the words and phrases they form are identical.

Image

Elsewhere in this book, we have used the word *image* to denote a composition within a motion graphic frame or sequence. However the strict sense of the word describes an optical likeness: a reflection, scan, photograph, or video recording. We are likely to make extensive use of "image" when discussing motion graphics since so much of the raw material is acquired this way. Images carry the communicative **denotation** of the object that they resemble, but we can break down the visual constituents of the image to abstract subelements, such as shape and value, if this helps us assess their structural contribution within the image or composition overall. For example, shadows in a high-contrast photograph that form a bold shape or pattern have the potential to strengthen or undermine the composition, depending on the visual interactions between this shape and the other design elements.

2.5 Sound: Making the unreal realistic
In this Bark and Bite film about Accuhealth's diabetes monitoring technology, a collection of colorful data parcels swarms about the screen, assembling into various shapes and forms. All the movement is created by 3D CGI animation, but it is the addition of sounds—whooshes and thuds— that imbues the parcels with plausible speed, weight, and personality.

www.barkandbite.com

Negative space

Space is what is left between elements, but it is as active as shape, line, type, or image. Space, too, can be placed and scaled by the reciprocal repositioning and scaling of the other elements that intrude into it. Space can be a very effective tool for creating order and emphasis.

Sound

Despite the emphasis on graphics in the nomenclature "motion graphics," we must remember that the aural can be as important as the visual in the work we create. *Sound* may take the form of speech, music, or sound effects. Sound effects may depict a natural occurrence in the real world, whether recorded or synthesized by the computer or another device. *Sound* effects may also be wholly unnatural in origin (e.g., whooshes, beeps, and pings that seem to translate the visual directly into the auditory). Sound has amplitude, pitch, and duration, and these few attributes can be varied infinitely in order to emphasize or counterpoint the visual.

2.5

TONE

There are only four things that a motion graphics sequence must contain. The first two define the spatial limits of what we observe: the *height* and *width* of the image frame. The third delimits the temporal experience; a motion graphic must have *duration*. The fourth requirement, which provides us with the minimal visual content inside this spatial and temporal container, is one of the key design elements—*tone*.

Tone describes the relationships and proportions of brightness and darkness in an image, and it is usually what we rely on the most in order to make sense of what we are seeing. This is because the tonal information—light, mid-tones, and shadows—conveys the dimension, texture, and depth of an object. When we look at the image of a face, it is the tonal information, not the color information, that allows us to distinguish the contours of the nose, the lips, and the bone structure. More iconic imagery, such as logos and type, also has an inherent tonal characteristic— light or dark—that delineates it from its surroundings, thereby giving it shape.

Histograms

Histograms can provide us with an objective measure of the tonal variety in an image or video sequence. Put simply, it is a bar graph that counts how many pixels possess a given tone.

The horizontal axis of the histogram is the spectrum of available shades, organized left-to-right from the lowest (black) to the highest (white), with the progressively brighter shades residing between these two extremes. The vertical axis of the histogram is a tally of the pixels present for each individual tone. Thus, a tall bar rising on the left of a histogram denotes an image with a large number of dark pixels; conversely, a tall bar rising on the far right of the histogram corresponds to a large number of consistently bright pixels found in various regions of the image.

A typical continuous-tone image that contains a diverse spectrum of tones would appear as a "mountain range" on the histogram; neighboring peaks and troughs corresponding to the varied shadows, mid-tones, and highlights.

Most semiprofessional camcorders and digital single lens reflex cameras (DSLRs) can display a histogram version of the image, which allows for an objective assessment of the contrast (or lack of contrast) concealed within the viewfinder image. In image editing and video compositing software, the histogram display acts as the user interface for tonal adjustments. A contrast adjustment is represented by a "squashing" or "stretching" of the histogram spectrum. A brightness adjustment is represented by shifting the peaks of bars farther up or down the horizontal axis.

Tone versus color

Tone and color are not mutually exclusive. Tone is evident in a color image just as it is in a grayscale image, such as a black-and-white photograph. In a full-color raster image, the primary colors (red, green, and blue) can be averaged to derive a brightness value. Thus, a dark red pixel would have a different hue from a dark blue pixel, but they may have identical tone.

Even when an image is bursting with vibrant hues, there is benefit in assessing its tonal qualities to reveal whether the colorful image is also utilizing the full spectrum of available tones.

Tone is not merely a byproduct of other elements. Like other elements such as line, shape, and type, tone is a property that we can selectively place and manipulate in order to create effective motion graphics.

2.6

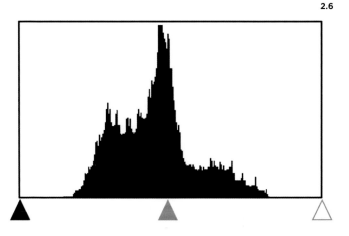

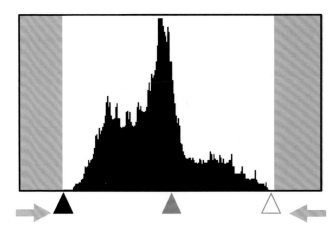

2.6 Histograms and tonal range

The meerkat image above (top) contains a variety of tone and color, but by displaying the image histogram, we can see that the image is mostly mid-tones, represented by a "mountain range" at the midrange of the histogram.

By sliding the light and dark limits to match the tonal range of the image (center), the histogram is expanded to fill the available spectrum, injecting more shadows and highlights into the meerkat image.

Bottom: The two histograms—before and after adjustment—are superimposed for comparison.

Please see www.bloomsbury.com/crook-motion-graphics for more on this project.

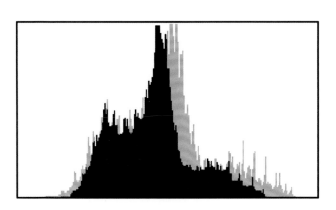

2.7
In this title sequence by
Momoco for the BBC adaptation
of *Great Expectations*, color is
subdued almost to the point of
elimination.

The reliance on tone gives
emphasis to the shape and
texture of the lace and the
butterfly wings. The delicate
imagery evokes the fragility of
the relationships in Dickens'
novel and the precariousness
of the hero's ascent in Victorian
society.

2.7

THE PIXEL

DESIGN
ELEMENTS

TONE

COLOR

RASTERS AND
VECTORS

TEXT AND
TYPE

DESIGN
PRINCIPLES

COLOR

Color is a crucial element in the majority of visual designs. Furthermore, color adjustment (or grading) has become an increasingly critical phase in enhancing and post-producing video material. If we properly understand how humans perceive and classify color, we can make many more strategic decisions about how the color elements of an image should be refined or adjusted. Similarly, if we understand how color is created and encoded in computer-based systems, then we will be able to map our notions of color into the editing environment.

What is color?

Color is the word we use to describe our visual experience of some types of electromagnetic radiation. A light source, such as the sun, radiates electromagnetic energy that is then partially absorbed or reflected when it reaches an object. Our eyes receive the reflected portion of the radiation and convert it from an electromagnetic signal to a chemical one, which in turn is converted to electrical impulses in our optic nerve.

Inside our eyes are different types of light receptors called rods and cones. The rods react to the amplitude of the light radiation; we recognize this as brightness or darkness. The cones are sensitive to the light radiation of low, mid, or high frequencies that correspond to our sensation of red, green, and blue. These three bands of color sensitivity define the primary colors. The primary colors combine to create the millions of colors that we perceive.

The different shades of green that we see when we gaze upon a meadow or forest are dependent upon these variable and compound frequencies of electromagnetic radiation that are absorbed or reflected when sunlight falls upon the grass. And, although most people would agree that grass is green, our sensation of color is entirely subjective.

2.8 The RGB color model
In the **RGB** model of color, maximum red, green, and blue light combine to create pure white (top). By selectively reducing the proportions of red, green, and blue, we can create millions of other colors, such as bright pink (center) or cyan (bottom).

Please see www.bloomsbury.com/crook-motion-graphics for more on this project.

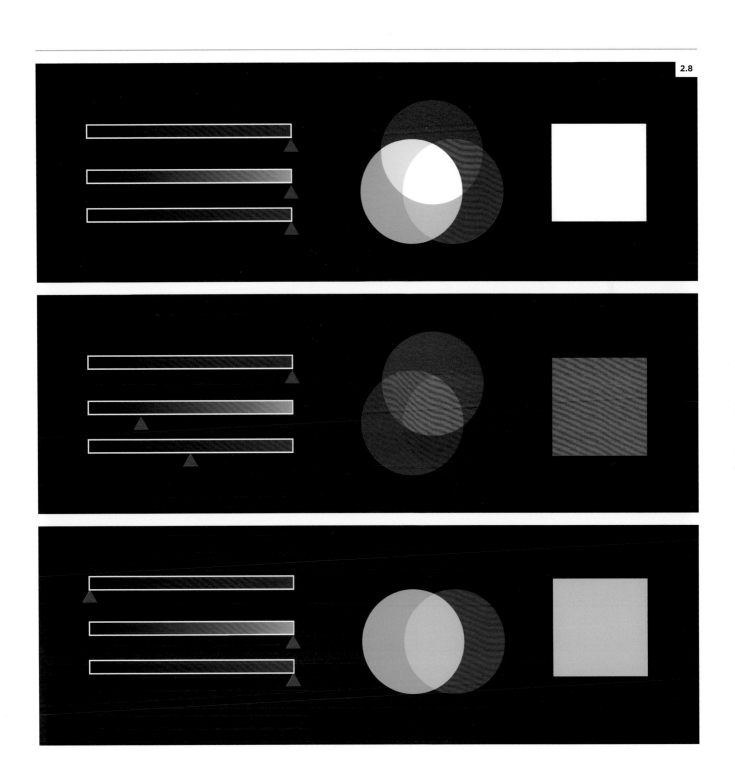

The human experience of color

Over centuries, artists and scientists have devised various models and concepts in order to standardize the classification of color. Whereas these experts may be able to faithfully declare the proportions of a primary color in, say, a given shade of purple, we are more likely to attempt to describe its "purpleness" rather than its relative "redness," "blueness," or "greenness." Hence, an intuitive way of describing the purple may be to describe its *hue*, *saturation*, and *brightness*.

Hue

Hue is a familiar concept to any child who can distinguish between the different colors of the rainbow. It describes the "palette" color; the hue of grass is green, the hue of a banana is yellow.

Our ability to communicate the differences between hues is determined by our shared vocabulary. For example, paint manufacturers have devised all sorts of evocative terms (e.g., "sand," "magnolia," "custard") to categorize subtly different hues of yellow.

Although hue is really a manifestation of a particular frequency of the spectrum of light, the available spectrum of hues can also be depicted as a "wheel" of color with each hue distinguishable by its location within a full 360-degree circle.

Saturation

Saturation describes the intensity or vibrancy of the color. It is the quality of "how much" of a particular color we see. A faded denim jacket possesses the same hue as a new denim jacket, but it has a different saturation. We might distinguish between the two jackets by describing the faded one as "pale" or "muted" whereas the new one may be described as "deep" or "rich." This difference in the "blueness" of both items is a quality of saturation.

2.9 The HSV color model
The same three colors as those shown in 2.8, this time expressed using the hue, saturation, and brightness model. Hue is often depicted as a color wheel, with red at the top. All other hues can then be expressed as a figure between 0 and 360 degrees. Technically, pure white (top) has no hue or saturation; it has only maximum brightness. Our bright pink (center) has a hue of 340 degrees, a medium saturation, and a high brightness value. Cyan (bottom) has a hue of approximately 190 degrees, a mid-saturation value, and a high brightness value.

2.9

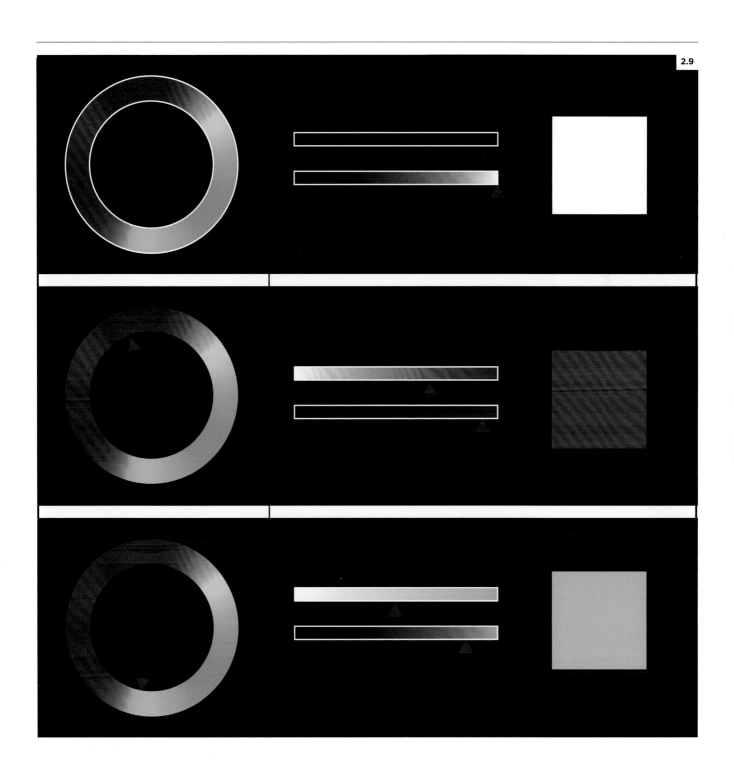

Brightness

Also known as the *value* of a color, *brightness* is the extent to which the hue and saturation may be affected by the overall tone (lightness or darkness) of an object. For example, imagine that you have two matching garden chairs, both a pale blue of identical hue and saturation. If you were to place one of the chairs in the direct path of the sun, it would appear to be a bright pale blue whereas the identical chair placed in the shadow of your house would appear to be a dark pale blue. Hence, brightness/value is related to the overall amount of light reflected or emitted, rather than the proportions of the color spectrum.

Using color

Although hue, saturation, and brightness are useful for classifying color, they do not provide us with a useful scheme for selecting and combining colors.

In order to deploy color effectively, we must first consider any intrinsic associations that a color creates in the mind of the audience. A color scheme may identifiably belong to the corporate identity of a product or service. Color may also exhibit archetypal meaning, such as red being used (in certain cultural contexts) to indicate danger, passion, or festivity. In these situations, color brings meaning with it.

In addition, we must consider the relationships between one color element and all other elements in the composition. Color harmony exists when the component colors have distinctly similar or contrasting hue, saturation, or brightness. There are a number of established relationships that yield harmonious color combinations, and there are a multitude of websites that explain these combinations and catalog color schemes (colourlovers.com is one example).

Color in the video display

Video displays (e.g., TVs and monitors) are similar to the raster images they show, in that they are comprised of tiny rows and columns. Each row contains hundreds of miniature light emitters organized into groups of three (triads) with a red, green, and blue emitter in each triad group. Similar to human vision, video signals (and the display technologies that transform these signals into images) regard color as a combination of the color primaries: red, green, and blue.

The numerical pixel data in the video file or transmission is translated into a continuous signal that scans rapidly across the screen and excites the rows of triads to emit the appropriate color. When excited in the correct proportions, the triads can reproduce one of many millions of possible colors, including pure white.

For a moving image to be displayed on a screen, the playback device (e.g., computer, TV, smartphone) must be capable of recreating millions of these tiny color elements in an objective and consistent way. Hence, a reference video signal of consistent hues and brightness is often supplied to the monitor so that it can be correctly calibrated.

Some monitors do not display mid-tones as faithfully as highlights and shadows. Consequently, many monitors have a **gamma** adjustment that calibrates the reaction of the triad emitters to tones and colors in the mid-part of the video signal.

2.10 Missguided

This advertisement, produced by Bark and Bite for clothing brand Missguided, demonstrates how a restricted color palette results in a slick and unified sequence that emphasizes the critical information or product.

www.barkandbite.com

2.10

RASTERS AND VECTORS

We have learned that the visual data that fills a frame of video is made up from an array of tiny pixels. Each pixel possesses a single color value that, when displayed alongside its neighbors, creates the appearance of consistent or variable color, texture, and shape across the full territory of the frame. The arrangement of pixels of different colors is what gives the image the appearance of variable color and tone that enables us to discern the people, objects, locations, and type that are depicted in the image.

When the image data is stored faithfully, the numerical data for each pixel is stored as a separate and distinct number value that belongs to the pixel. When this faithful per-pixel data is reconstituted into a complete image, the entire array of pixels is known as a **raster image**.

However, computers are capable of expressing and storing visual data in an alternative way. These are descriptions of shapes called **vector images**.

Describing shapes

Consider the flag of the Republic of Cameroon: a yellow star in the center of three vertical bands of green, red, and yellow. Although we may conceptualize this as only a few limited geometrical shapes possessing different dimensions and colors, we understand that when the image data is saved as a raster image file there are a multitude of elements required to create the appearance of these finite shapes. However, it is possible for the computer to save this visual data in a manner that is much more analogous to our perception of a single star in front of three colored rectangles.

If the computer regards the image frame as a canvas of defined dimensions, it can store the coordinates of the uppermost corners of each of the three rectangles, as well as their height, width, and color, in addition to the 10 coordinates that are joined to reveal the star. This approach—known as an *object-oriented* approach to describing visual data— is a much more efficient method of expressing the same visual data that would be contained in an equivalent raster image. Instead of stipulating the color characteristics of many thousands of pixels, we need to know the characteristics of only four shape objects—admittedly of varied height, width, shape, and position.

2.11

2.11 Describing shapes
The flag of the Republic of Cameroon contains four distinct geometric shapes in three colors. Vector formats can store simple geometrical information like this in a very efficient way.

Vector images

Image file formats that use this object-oriented method of describing and storing a set of geometric shapes and coordinates are called vector image files. Whereas a raster image is displayed by "streaming" the pixels row by row, the vector image is displayed by "drawing" the shapes, one upon the other. Any element that can be expressed by means of fixed or calculated coordinates can be understood by a vector image. Rectangles, triangles, ellipses, lines, and curves are common inhabitants of vector images, but type too can be expressed as a combination of varied shapes, lines, and curves. Hence, type formats are usually a form of vector file.

Adobe Illustrator (**AI**) is widely used for creating and editing elegant vector images. Most video-editing or compositing software will also feature an integrated vector-editing environment for adding shapes and type to a video sequence. Boris FX is one such tool that can be found in many nonlinear editing and compositing software from Apple, Adobe, and Avid.

Scalability

Vector images are very convenient for computers to manipulate. Resizing a vector image is a simple matter of scaling the dimensions; of recalculating and replotting the coordinates. By contrast, resizing a raster image requires the creation of lots of new pixels; the computer has to rely on guesswork to estimate the color that these new pixels should inherit.

Similarly, rotating a vector image requires only an adjustment of several key coordinates, whereas rotating a raster image involves shuffling hundreds, possibly thousands, of pixels to a new position in the raster grid.

Naturally, there are some types of visual information that it would be impossible to articulate as a vector image. A face does not contain a finite number of geometric shapes; it is comprised of multiple, subtly different tones that delimit the various contours we recognize as facial features. This type of continuous tone image will be better expressed as a raster image.

Part of the skill of motion graphic design is recognizing which types of visual image are best expressed as vectors and which are best expressed as rasters. If we get it wrong, the consequences may be oversized files, lengthy downloads, redundant processing demands, or loss of image fidelity.

2.12

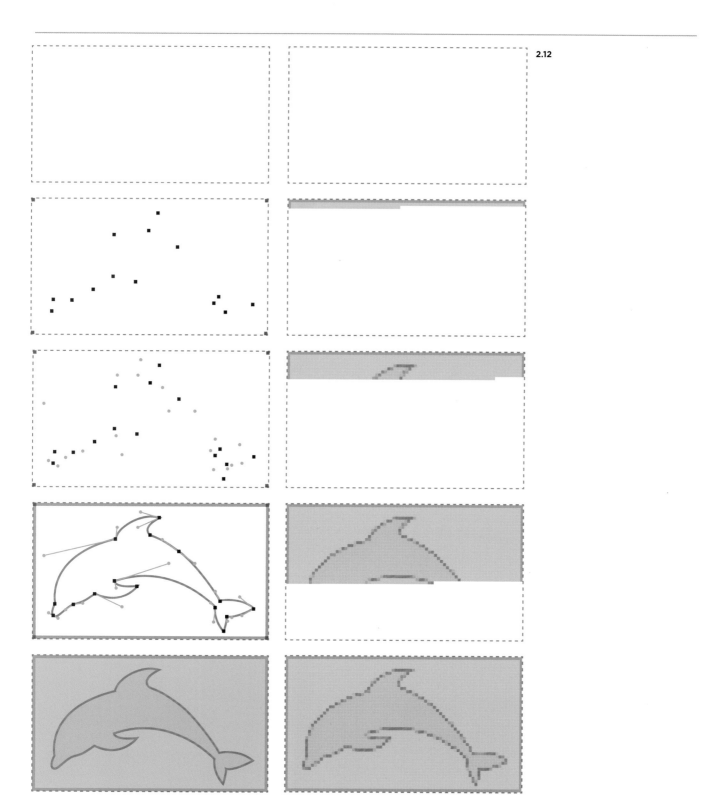

Rasterization

Because vector images are comprised of data that precisely describes contours, coordinates, and geometry, they are independent of an underlying grid structure that characterizes the raster canvas of photographs or video.

It is always necessary for the geometrically precise outline of a vector image to be transformed into a collection of pixels so that it can reside in the raster matrix of the video frame. This process is called *rasterization*. Most image- and video-editing software will spontaneously and effortlessly rasterize vector shapes for display purposes, but revert to the vector characteristics if the object or type requires scaling or repositioning. Rasterization is permanent, however, when the final sequence is exported or published as a movie.

Anti-aliasing

Rasterization is analogous to pressing a pancake into an ice-cube tray. Each "hollow" pixel "compartment" in the underlying grid is "filled" with a value from the overlying vector shape. However, if the contour of the vector (the perimeter of a circle, for example) bisects rather than wholly covers a pixel in the raster grid, then there is no option to create a pixel that is "part filled in." As a result, the smooth curves or diagonals of the vector are constrained to a rather blocky "staircase" of pixels.

This problem is called *aliasing*, and is an issue with even high-resolution raster images and high-definition video. It occurs because the pixel grid is too coarse a structure to allow for the smooth curves of the vector to be resolved.

However, it is possible to reduce the apparent blocky-ness of vectors in a raster image. The boundary pixels can be filled with a value of a mid-tone, rather than the full-tone sampled from the vector shape. Although the rigid horizontals and verticals of the raster grid are still present, the outcome is an apparently smoother outline. This process is called *anti-aliasing*, and is a "number-crunching" exercise performed automatically by the computer to derive intermediate pixel values for the problematic regions of the vector.

2.12 The anatomy of vectors and rasters
Vectors and rasters use different concepts to build similar visual data. In the left-hand column, we see the anatomy of a vector image. First, the image territory is declared (top). Next, the primary coordinates are positioned; these will be the "dots" that are joined to create various shapes and lines. Additional coordinates are added; these "handles" are the tension points that determine the curvature of the primary lines. Next, the points are joined with a line of declared weight and color, and enclosed shapes are filled with color to finalize the shapes that comprise the image (bottom).

By comparison, in the right-hand column we see a raster image building: a stream of colored pixels that assemble like building blocks, one after the other. The color value of each successive pixel is rapidly decoded and displayed until the entire image territory is filled in. The colored mosaic that results can be resolved in fine or coarse detail, depending on the resolution of the image.

Please see www.bloomsbury.com/crook-motion-graphics for more on this project.

TEXT AND TYPE

Text is an important element in motion graphics, as it often relays much of the information: for example, names, figures, dates, instructions, and other key messages. The *text* of *Alice in Wonderland*—the words used to tell the story—will be the same regardless of the edition you read, but the *type*—the specific arrangement of ink on paper—may differ from imprint to imprint. Whereas text refers to the linguistic content of the collection of words, type refers to the graphical "container": the optional shape and style of the letterforms that imbues a word or phrase with a personality that is independent of the semantics of that word or phrase.

Typography

Writing effective text (also called *copy*) is a key skill because the medium is characterized by temporality of words on a screen of limited dimensions. Therefore, as motion graphic designers, we may be working with words and messages carefully written by somebody else. Our role may be to add to the message by the strategic deployment of the design element of type.

Placing type in a design is a sophisticated practice that involves more than identifying which font has the most apposite "feel." *Typography*—the craft of selecting, combining, and arranging type—also considers how the type is set into the available space. Typography involves specifying the size, color, and position of the letterforms, as well as the amount of negative space between lines, words, and characters. The expert typographer recognizes that type is an intricate assemblage of diverse shapes, lines, and spaces with the capacity to introduce harmony or discord to a motion graphic. Motion graphic designers should be cultured in the elegant use of type and can put to good use the many excellent books on the subject. Several highly recommended titles are listed in the appendix.

TIP | TYPE SIZE

Type size is specified with an antiquated unit of measure called a *point*. A point is defined as 1/72 of 1 inch. The point size of a font does not describe the height of the letterform, however. The height of a font also includes an enclosure of negative space above and below the letterforms.

Fonts

Although *typeface* and *font* are often used interchangeably, digital typographers make a distinction between the two terms to avoid ambiguity. A typeface describes the appearance of an alphabet of letterforms in a consistent style. Familiar typefaces are Times New Roman and Arial. Comic Sans is another (often maligned) example. A font, on the other hand, is the piece of computer software that allows the typeface to be rendered by a computer screen or printer. On a Mac or PC, the most common file format for a font is the TrueType standard, recognizable by the file extension ".ttf."

A TrueType font is a directory of vector files that describes how to outline each letterform for every corresponding press of the keyboard. The vector format means that the smooth curves of the letterforms are preserved regardless of the size at which the type is created.

Type and copyright

Digital fonts are protected by a variety of international laws that govern how and where they may be used. In some countries, there are restrictions on how and where you may use the software that renders the typeface (i.e., the letterforms). Elsewhere in the world, it is not only the font software but also the shape of the letters that is protected. As digital designers, we must respect the type as property of the original typographer or foundry. It is vital to check that we have permission to use the type as we plan. This permission is usually explicit in the software license that accompanies the digital font.

Anti-aliasing and moving type

Because a font is a vector image, it must be rasterized for display in a composition or movie. That is, it is necessary to transform the vector outline of a letterform into pixels so that it can reside in the raster matrix of the video frame. Anti-aliasing is required so that the appearance of smooth curves is preserved across the strict horizontals and verticals of the raster grid.

Although anti-aliasing occurs behind the scenes, it is important to monitor how effectively it is handled. Typefaces with very delicate features, such as thin lines or elaborate curls and scrolls, may be too fine to be adequately resolved on the raster grid, even with anti-aliasing enabled. As a result, parts of the type may seem truncated or absent. Similarly, as type moves across the raster grid, the anti-aliasing may produce fluctuating results, which could create the appearance of "flashing" or "throbbing" letterforms.

Modern type foundries (the visual designers and software manufacturers who create the electronic fonts) are aware of these problems and design many typefaces specifically to avoid screen-based defects.

2.13

2.13 To do list

This short personal project by Yaniv Fridman and Daniel Luna makes great use of simple images and beautiful type to convey a message of life choices.

The letterforms are created from a variety of typefaces that work harmoniously with the images to tell the story. Each font has been carefully matched to its sequence.

In the case of the bike sequence, the typeface has been distorted to make it seem as if it is a bicycle inner tube.

DESIGN PRINCIPLES

As motion graphic designers, we can regard design elements (e.g., color, shape, line, type) as our building materials. Design *principles*, on the other hand, constitute a variety of assembly guidelines that we can adapt in order to arrange and combine these materials.

We may find that one arrangement (we could also use the word *composition*) is more or less pleasing than another. Recognizing which of the design principles are in use can be a crucial method for diagnosing design problems. If we understand the design principles that result in different compositions, then we may better assess and articulate how one design is preferable to another.

Alignment

Alignment is a strong way to create the appearance of order in a composition. If the edges or centers of several elements are positioned so that they appear to be in a consistent line, then we have aligned these elements.

Symmetry and balance

Symmetry creates the illusion that one half of an image (or a set of elements within it) is the reflection of the other half. Each element has a corresponding partner on the opposing side of the composition. Symmetry is one method of creating balance in a composition, but balance may also be achieved by pairing dissimilar elements, or partnering lone elements with groups of elements. For example, a composition that has a large circle at its upper left may be balanced by a cluster of smaller squares at the bottom right. Although the image is not symmetrical, balance is nevertheless achieved.

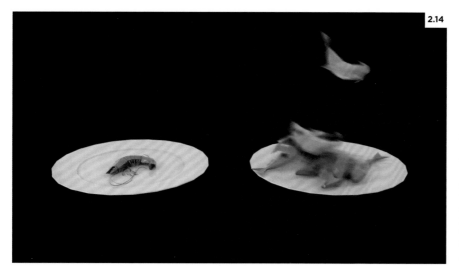

2.14

2.14 The use of asymmetry to create meaning
The Overfishing of the Ocean and *F-Gases* are two short films by Uli Henrik Streckenbach of Uhsless Design. They combine voice narration with animated graphics in order to convey alarming facts about environmental issues. The films make considerable and impressive use of visual design principles to convey statistics with impact, and to make the consequences of industrial practices more relevant.

www.uhsless.de

Direction

An element in an image sequence may appear to move in a given direction across the frame by means of animation, but static images can also possess direction via the strategic placement of tone, line, type, or shape. Single or converging lines can imply direction, as can shapes, such as triangles and arrows. Tonal variation, such as a transition from light to dark, may also lead the eye across the frame, creating direction. Type has an inherent direction—the direction in which it is read—but this path is not necessarily horizontal, left-to-right, as seen in the glut of recent **kinetic type** infographics.

Proportion

Proportion describes the relationships of relative height, width, depth, area, volume, distance, and (in our context of time-based design) duration. Effective and pleasing proportion is apparent even in a single element. A rectangle, for example, possesses a height-to-width relationship.

For many centuries, artists and designers have favored the ubiquitous proportion known as the *golden mean* (also known as the *golden section* or the *golden ratio*), which is a ratio of 1:1.618. The golden mean is evident in works of art and natural formations such as flowers, shells, and storms. It can also be found in the relative dimensions of our own limbs and faces.

Figure/ground

In a two-dimensional image, all elements exist on a flat image plane; no element can protrude from the canvas and no image can recede beyond the image plane. *Figure/ground* describes the way in which one element may appear to sit above other elements on this plane. It is possible to create strong figure/ground relationships by using contrasts in tone or color, or by the implied continuation of partially hidden elements. For example, most viewers will assume that a solid square is obscured rather than dissected by a circle that sits on one of its corners.

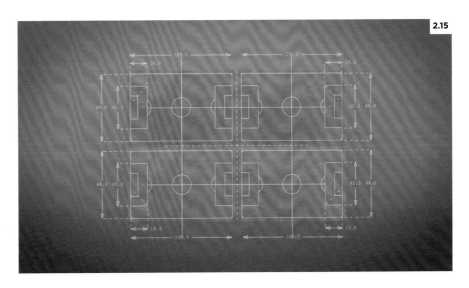

2.15

2.15 The use of alignment for unity
Strong alignment organizes and unifies rectangular elements on the screen. The "four football pitches" illustrates, in understandable terms, the surface area of industrial fishing nets.

Symmetry and contrast are used to make a visual comparison between industrial fishing yields and their corresponding wastes.

www.uhsless.de

Position

Each elemental member of a composition must occupy a position relative to the boundary of the frame, and relative to each other. In addition, elements may appear to possess a position relative to the vantage point of the viewer. They may seem to be close or distant, depending on their scale or figure/ground relationships.

The extent to which elements appear to be grouped or separated is determined by position and the resulting residue of space. Adjacent elements will appear to be grouped or related; elements separated by a greater margin will appear disconnected or unrelated, unless they are similar in other ways.

Similarity

The extent to which elements are similar influences our perception of whether or not they are unified. Thus, two elements, segregated by other elements such as line or space, may appear to belong together if they have a common color, trajectory, or figure/ground index.

Contrast

Contrast can be created by using opposing colors or tones, by alternating directions, or by extremes of scale. In general, it is a good principle to utilize high or low contrast in your composition: elements must be *perfectly similar* or *distinctly different*, because subtle differences may look like defects.

Contrast, like all the other principles we have encountered, is equally applicable to the element of sound. Sound may exhibit contrasting attributes such as amplitude, pitch, and duration.

2.16

2.16 Rhythm through sound and image
More exemplars of design principles from Uli Henrik Streckenbach. In colorful bands, a number of objects appear on screen, each one a source of fluorinated greenhouse gases, a cause of climate change. The slicing of the screen into portions creates visual rhythm; the effect is emphasized by the rhythmic clattering of metallic sounds.

www.uhsless.de

Rhythm

Rhythm is created by the repetition of similar elements. Parallel lines separated by equal divisions, for example, can create a rhythm across a composition. Rows or columns of repeated shapes can create a pattern, which is a variation of rhythm. In time-based design, the appearance or disappearance of elements may also create a temporal rhythm.

2.17 Circles, the motion graphic designer's friend
Similar shapes recur through Uli's environmental films. A circular motif unifies many of the separate scenes in the films. Circles contrast very strongly with the rectangular canvas of the screen, which may be one of the reasons that the simple shape proliferates in motion graphics.

www.uhsless.de

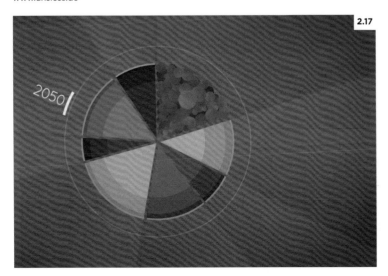

2.17

Discord

Combinations of elements can be described as discordant if they appear to conflict (i.e., to disregard any of the other principles described here). Discord is usually undesirable—the consequence of poor composition. However, discord may sometimes be a conscious design choice rather than a mistake. For example, an asymmetrical image that has a lot of negative space on one side may appear to be an incomplete composition. But as we are dealing with time-based composition, this discord can create in the mind of the viewer anticipation that the balance will be restored. The desire for harmony will motivate the arrival of, say, text or graphics to fill the apparent void. Thus, with the selective use of discord, we have the potential to design-in tension.

Change

The marvel of motion graphics is that not one of the principles described in this section must be permanent. In a static image, composition is fixed, but in an animated sequence, composition may evolve. We can author a sequence so that any element may change its color, shape, size, or position.

Change may occur relative to the initial appearance of the element itself; for example, a circle may grow, shrink, spin, fall, float, fade, glow, pulse, or morph into a square. Alternatively, change may occur relative to other elements within the frame; the circle may evolve while a twin remains the same. This means that the power of a composition will be affected not only when elements change, but also when they stay the same.

Consequently, the craft of motion graphics, as opposed to, say, poster design, is defined by the extent to which we exploit—or deny—the potential for change.

By changing the characteristics of an element we can imbue it with behaviors that extend beyond the visual: a slow-moving object has apparent mass, a fast-moving element possesses power, a change in size may imply an approach toward or a recession from the image plane. It is not an overstatement to claim that by selectively deploying and adjusting design principles we can bring images to life.

CHAPTER THREE
CONCEPTS:
SPACE

In the real world everything exists within a three-dimensional space. An object has properties of height, width, and depth. In the world of motion graphics we have total control over each of these dimensions and can manipulate these properties to achieve certain results.

In this chapter we will look at the virtual and physical placing of objects and how they interact with the screen and hence the viewer. We will discover the language and vocabulary used to describe objects in space. We will explore dimensionality as understood by the computer. We will learn how to think and work in two, two and a half, three, and stereoscopic three dimensions. We will explore the use of fully immersive environments and the impact they have on motion graphics. Finally, we will consider the physical screen dimensions that we have to work within.

By the end of this chapter you should have a full understanding of space and how you can use and manipulate it.

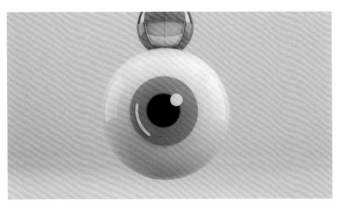
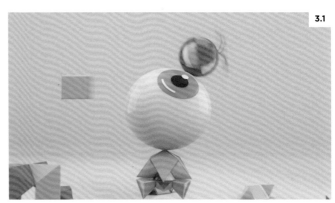

3.1 *The Zone*
In this sequence from Tendril the colorful objects fly and bounce around the screen. Even though there is no discernible scenery, the use of depth, placing some objects in the foreground and others far in the background, gives a tangible experience of space.

www.tendril.ca

ASPECT RATIO

Conventionally (but not exclusively), images and movies are experienced on a rectangular canvas, screen, or display. Aspect ratio describes the size relationship of the height and width of this canvas. Aspect ratio is typically expressed as two numbers, width followed by height, separated by a colon (e.g., 4:3). The numbers are purely relative, meaning that they represent completely arbitrary but consistent divisions, rather than fixed units such as millimeters or pixels.

Whatever the actual dimensions of the canvas may be, it is conventional to scale down the height and width values to their lowest common whole-number denominators in order to express the aspect ratio. This allows us to recognize when display contexts of different physical dimensions may share the same height-to-width relationship.

For example, the display area of a smartphone may have physical dimensions of 45mm wide and 75mm high, with a corresponding pixel array of 480 × 800 pixels. The aspect ratio of this would not be expressed as 45:75, or 480:800, but would be expressed as the smallest proportional whole numbers, which in this case would be 3:5. High-definition TVs come in many different sizes, but they are largely the same shape, possessing a common aspect ratio of 16:9. Other common aspect ratios are 4:3 (the proportions of standard-definition TV, as well as the iPad), 3:2 (found on earlier generation smartphones), and 1:1, which is a square.

An alternative method of expressing aspect ratio is to denote the shorter value as precisely 1. Our smartphone example would therefore be expressed as 1:1.6.

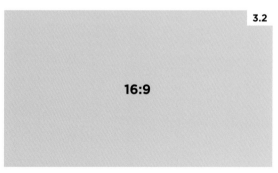

3.2

3.2 Landscape or portrait
We do not need to take aspect ratio for granted, as most portable devices, although fixed in dimensions, can be rotated by the user. In film and television, the convention has been for moving images to be short and wide: a landscape orientation (above). However, in recent years it has been possible to mount large, lightweight video monitors in a landscape or portrait (left) orientation. By rotating the traditional television screen by 90 degrees to create a tall and thin canvas, new possibilities have arisen. For example, this aspect ratio is much better suited to motion graphics relating to the upright human figure, such as in fashion and health.

ASPECT
RATIO

DESCRIBING
OBJECTS   2D   2.5   IMMERSIVE AND CASE STUDY:
IN SPACE   MOTION   DIMENSIONS   3D CGI   STEREOSCOPIC AUGMENTED   MAKE
                                                             3D   ENVIRONMENTS   PRODUCTIONS

Aspect ratio conversion

Aspect ratio conversion occurs when an image of one aspect ratio is adjusted to fit a screen or display of conflicting dimensions. As a result, the image may distort (stretch or squeeze); the image may crop undesirably, omitting visual information from the boundaries of the composition; or the image may be displayed with margins added to the top and bottom (known as *letterboxing*), to the left and right sides (*pillar-boxing*), or to all edges (*window-boxing*). Sometimes this conversion can be managed, and the least destructive adjustment can be selected, but often aspect-ratio conversion is an inadvertent consequence of delivering a video sequence to the wrong specifications. As screen space is a valuable commodity, we should strive to ensure that it is used to its full potential.

Landscape versus portrait

When the width of a canvas is greater than the height, this is described as a *landscape* orientation, reflecting the conventional proportions of a classical painting of a landscape. Conversely, a canvas that is taller than it is wide is described as *portrait* orientation. For a long time, display technologies were so bulky that we would never have considered rotating them to provide an alternative aspect ratio. The landscape display was de facto. Portrait designs were the preserve of posters and print publications. However, an iPad display will possess an aspect ratio of either 4:3 or 3:4 depending on which way up it is being held. Furthermore, although TV shows and films continue to be produced in a landscape format, this conventional orientation of a TV display is being challenged in certain environments, such as retail, where it is not unusual to exploit a vertical screen instead of a horizontal one if it provides a fuller display of goods or services.

Aspect ratio is an important consideration in designing any graphic, whether it is moving or static. You may be authoring a moving image on a desktop computer that will ultimately be projected onto a cinema screen or even the side of a building. Whereas the fixed dimensions of the display may vary depending on the context of the viewing, the aspect ratio describes a scalable canvas or fixed proportions within which our design elements are placed. As moving images emerge in more and more environments on more varied devices, aspect ratio is a key criterion.

DESCRIBING OBJECTS IN SPACE

Throughout this section we will see that it is important that we are able to accurately describe where an object is in space. In the real world this is second nature. We see the pen on the table in front of us. We know where it is so precisely through years of experience that we can pick it up with very little difficulty.

When creating motion graphics, however, we are no longer in the real world. We are in an artificial, virtual world. Being able to say where things are is more difficult. This means we have to have a set of terms that enables us to accurately refer to objects so that we know where they are in relation to the viewer and to each other.

To ensure that we can find objects we use a set of coordinates known as X, Y, and Z.

X, Y axes

The X and Y coordinates should be familiar to anyone who has ever studied a graph. The horizontal axis is referred to as the *X axis* and the vertical axis is known as the *Y axis*. A simple way to remember is that X is "a cross"!

An object on a plane will have a position that is made up of two numbers. These numbers describe how far left or right we are along the horizontal X axis and how far up or down we are along the vertical Y axis.

Coordinates

An object's position in space is referred to as an *X,Y coordinate*. Depending on the system you are using, the coordinate could be a simple whole number or, in a more complex system, multiple decimal places of accuracy. Regardless of how accurate the numbers are, there are some important points to bear in mind.

The first is that you need to know the position of the origin. This is the point 0,0 (0 on the X axis and 0 on the Y axis). Usually, this will be in the top left-hand corner of the screen or the workspace you are working in. This is not always the case though—it could be at the center of the screen or anywhere else one chooses to set it—so you need to check. If you do not know, however, it is generally safe to assume that it will be in the top left.

The second point to remember is that the values on the X axis will increase as you move from left to right. In the Western world this seems logical as that is the way we read and the way that graphs are typically displayed. Values on the Y axis, however, increase as you move from top to bottom. If you are thinking of your display like a graph, this may be counterintuitive.

The Z axis

We can create the illusion of depth by introducing a third dimension. This is known as the *Z axis* and is a virtual plane that goes in and out from the screen. Objects that move along the Z axis will appear to get larger as the Z coordinate increases and smaller as the Z coordinate decreases. Despite the fact that the screen is two dimensional, this approach tricks our eye into believing that the objects are able to move in and out of the screen, thereby creating the illusion of three dimensionality.

It is important to remember that the X, Y, and Z coordinates are not only relative to the geometry of the entire environment but also to each individual object. Hence, the effect of moving a cube along its X axis could give the impression that it is moving in and out of the screen, depending on the orientation of our main view. At times you may see the Z axis bar running horizontally across the screen rather than receding away from the surface plane of the display. This is because we are able to reorientate the whole virtual space relative to the viewing plane.

We learned in an earlier section about the characteristics of a camera lens, and how the focal length of the lens can affect the focus and perspective of an object that recedes from our vantage point. We can simulate this in our virtual camera.

Adjusting the focal length of the virtual camera has the effect of stretching the Z axis. This means that the perspective of the object is changed when we are viewing the scene with the Z axis running in and out of the screen. This way we can also create the illusion of depth of field.

3.3

3.3 Isometric Z depth
This short film from Uhsless that explains land use and soil erosion makes good use of the Z axis. The sequence is designed around an isometric grid. Objects build up by flying in along the X, Y, and Z axes, providing a real sense of depth.

2D MOTION

When, as children, we first began to create images, our world existed on one flat plane. The ground was at the bottom of the page, the sky was at the top, and everything else was in between. If we drew a house with a car outside, invariably the car would be drawn to one side, and only rarely in front.

We were thinking and working on one physical plane—in only two dimensions. Things can be positioned either up or down and left or right. In the art world before the fourteenth century, prior to the development of perspective, this was the predominant way of representing the world.

When working in two dimensions, commonly referred to as *2D*, we need to be able to orient ourselves so that we know where we are. Therefore, each point in space, each position of our object, has a set of X and Y coordinates. Each point then is referenced as a position on the X and a position on the Y. As we've already seen, this is usually written as X,Y.

Animating in 2D

Creating motion in two dimensions is simply a case of increasing or decreasing the values of the X and Y coordinates. A move across the screen from left to right will see the X value increasing. A move up the screen from the bottom will see the Y value decreasing. A diagonal move from the bottom right-hand corner of the screen will see both the X and the Y values decreasing.

The angle that an object moves diagonally is determined by how much you increase or decrease the X and Y values in relation to each other. If they are both altered by the same value, the object will move at 45 degrees. The exact angle can be calculated using trigonometry (remember "SohCahToa" from math class); however, unless you are programming your motion using code, you will not need to work this out yourself.

Saul Bass—2D pioneer

One of the greatest and earliest proponents of 2D motion graphics was Saul Bass (1920–1996). Born in New York, he was a graphic designer responsible for many internationally recognized logos, but his motion graphic film titles brought him to the public's attention. Beginning with the title sequence to Otto Preminger's *The Man With The Golden Arm* (1955), he used his experience with typography and contemporary design to produce stark graphic sequences that exquisitely captured the essence of the film. These were unlike anything seen on screen before.

His collaboration with Preminger and Alfred Hitchcock on the title sequences for *Anatomy of a Murder* (1958), *Vertigo* (1958), *North By Northwest* (1959), and *Psycho* (1960) set a style that was to be emulated often. His work was more recently rediscovered by director Martin Scorsese who persuaded him to create the title sequences for *Goodfellas* (1990), *Cape Fear* (1991), and his final sequence in *Casino* (1995). Bass is regarded as one of the premier exponents of the movie title sequence and is often cited as an influence to many of today's designers.

ASPECT
RATIO

DESCRIBING
OBJECTS
IN SPACE

2D
MOTION

2.5
DIMENSIONS

3D CGI

STEREOSCOPIC
3D

IMMERSIVE AND
AUGMENTED
ENVIRONMENTS

CASE STUDY:
MAKE
PRODUCTIONS

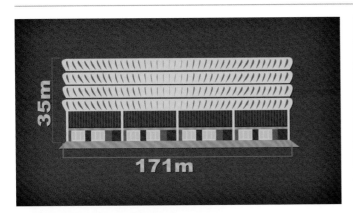

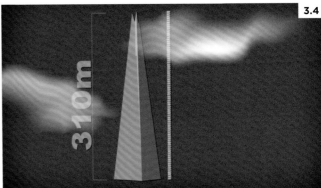

3.4

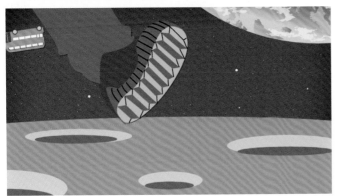

3.4 *Preston Bus Station*

This short, informative motion graphic by Richard Johnson gives details of the iconic bus station in the city of Preston, UK. The use of simple flat images, reminiscent of paper cutouts, ensures that the information is clearly communicated in an engaging manner.

The shots here show some of the physical dimensions of the building, the number of buses that use it, the year it was built, and the campaign to save it from demolition by securing it the status of "listed building."

2.5 DIMENSIONS

There is a technique of producing an illusion of depth in a moving image that takes the motion out of the purely two-dimensional realm while not being fully three dimensional. This is called *2.5 dimensional* (**2.5D**).

Imagine an image on screen of an old photograph. The virtual camera begins to move across the image from left to right. What initially looked like a 2D image now looks 3D as the objects in the foreground pass in front of the camera more quickly than objects in the middle ground, which in turn pass faster than objects in the background. This phenomenon is known as **parallax**.

The effect is somewhat akin to looking at a series of flat cutout images spaced in front of each other, like a shoebox theater. There is a sense of depth and flatness at the same time.

Image preparation

In order to produce the source material suitable for a 2.5D film, a separate image is needed for each level of the final sequence. If you are creating this all from scratch, the only thing that you need to ensure is that each layer, apart from the background, has some transparency around the object so that the layers behind can be seen through it.

If you are working on an already existing 2D image then you need to prepare it beforehand. Using an image-editing program, reproduce the source image as many times as there are object layers. Then isolate the foreground layers with transparency around the objects. For the background layer you need to remove the foreground elements, replacing them with new imagery. This could be done by cloning areas of the image to seamlessly hide the foreground objects. Alternatively, new objects (e.g., plants, furniture) could be blended over to hide the gaps.

Depth of field

The illusion can be further heightened by simulating *depth of field*. That is to say that we can create an area that is in focus. Objects farther forward or farther behind this area will appear blurred. We might have the object in the foreground in sharp focus, but have the objects in the background in various degrees of blurriness. This will strengthen the illusion of depth and provide the opportunity to highlight the subject.

We can use this technique creatively by altering the focus point. If we have the object in the foreground in focus at first and then over time progressively blur it out while sharpening the objects in the background, we effectively move the focus from one object to another. In film terms this is known as *pull focus*.

3.5 *Bank of Arizona*
This example from Make Productions shows the number of individual objects and layers that go into one simple sequence.

Each flat object is oriented at different points along the Z axis, creating the illusion of depth.

A considered use of depth of field completes the feeling that this is a real scene.

www.makeproductions.co.uk

3.5

ASPECT
RATIO

DESCRIBING
OBJECTS
IN SPACE

2D
MOTION

**2.5
DIMENSIONS**

3D CGI

STEREOSCOPIC
3D

IMMERSIVE AND
AUGMENTED
ENVIRONMENTS

CASE STUDY:
MAKE
PRODUCTIONS

Early pioneers

The 2.5D technique was introduced to a wide audience through the 2002 film *The Kid Stays in the Picture* by Nanette Burstein and Brett Morgen. The film is an adaptation of the autobiography of legendary film producer Robert Evans. It was mostly made up of a series of archive photographs. The photographs were animated with a series of slow movements into, out from, or across the images but utilizing the 2.5D technique to separate out the elements. This gave the impression that the images were more than simply static photographs. Occasionally they were combined with moving footage to further heighten the effect.

3D coordinate systems

Images that are said to be two dimensional exist along two planes or axes. The X axis is the horizontal, left to right, plane. The Y axis is the vertical, up and down, plane. Computers, TVs, and cinema screens are flat surfaces and are therefore two-dimensional planes.

As we've seen, we can create the illusion of depth by introducing a third dimension. This is known as the Z axis and is a virtual plane that goes in and out from the screen. Objects that move along the Z axis will appear to get larger as the Z coordinate increases and smaller as the Z coordinate decreases. Despite the fact that the screen is two dimensional, this approach tricks our eye into believing that the objects are able to move in and out of the screen and thus creates the illusion of three dimensionality.

3D CGI

3D *CGI* (*computer-generated imagery*) has become ubiquitous on screens worldwide, used in films, advertising, and music videos to such an extent that it is often confused for "real" film.

One of the first uses of 3D CGI in a film was called *A Computer Animated Hand* (1972), produced by Ed Catmull and Fred Parke at the University of Utah. It features a model of a hand that rotates, flexes, and points. The short sequence became the first 3D CGI to appear in a film in *Futureworld* (1976). Catmull went on to become one of the leading pioneers of CGI and was one of the founders of Pixar.

The main process in creating a CGI sequence is to make a model of an object in the computer, color it, add virtual lighting and cameras, and then take a series of shots of it. All CGI, no matter how photorealistic or graphically stylized, follows this same procedure.

Modeling

After an initial, paper-based design stage, the majority of CGI projects begin with modeling. This is the point that the underlying geometry of the model is created. A model is a collection of *vertices*, which are simply points in three-dimensional space (each with an X, Y, and Z coordinate). These points are joined by lines that in turn connect to make polygonal *faces*. This type of modeling is the most common and is referred to as *polygonal modeling*.

Because it is made up of straight lines it is not always easy to represent curved surfaces using polygonal modeling. Often many polygons are required, which drains computing power.

A similar process can be undertaken using curves rather than straight lines. Curves are capable of producing more organic shapes. These curved shapes are commonly known as *splines* or sometimes *NURBS* (non-uniform rational B-splines).

Digital sculpting

Digital sculpting is a process in CGI that has recently become common for producing highly realistic, organic models. The process begins with a simple polygon model. The model is then worked on in the sculpting software to manipulate the polygons. They can be expanded, contracted, pulled, pinched, textured, and smoothed, as if the model was a piece of clay. The action creates more polygons on the model through a process called *subdivision*. This leads to the name *high poly modeling*. An example of free modeling software is Autodesk Mudbox (www.autodesk.com /products/mudbox).

| ASPECT RATIO | DESCRIBING OBJECTS IN SPACE | 2D MOTION | 2.5 DIMENSIONS | | STEREOSCOPIC 3D | IMMERSIVE AND AUGMENTED ENVIRONMENTS | CASE STUDY: MAKE PRODUCTIONS |

3D CGI

Rigging

If the modeled object is going to have internal movement (e.g., a moving arm or some other joint), rather than simply changing position on screen, it is going to need some form of skeleton to tell it how and where to move. A digital skeleton, or rig, is created rather like the armatures used in professional stop-motion puppets. This consists of a series of bones that are connected by joints that have restrictions on how and where they can bend.

The rig sits inside the model and the "bones" are associated with different areas of the polygon object. When the rig is moved, the polygon model then follows suit. This way the model can be placed into various poses.

3.6 *Peseta*
These stills from a charming film by Uhsless on European climate change demonstrate a stylized approach to 3D CGI. The European Union headquarters and the polar bear on the ice are both recognizable but have been rendered in a particularly flat and angular way. The bear, however, is rigged so that it can be animated in a lifelike manner.

Animating

Once the model has been placed on the stage, lit by virtual lights, and framed by the virtual camera, the actual process of animation is basically the same as traditional animation using a combination of key-framing and tweening. The model to be animated is placed in a starting position on one frame, the frame indicator is then moved forward, and the object is repositioned into the new position. The computer works out the intermediary positions.

If the model is rigged, this may also mean setting a series of poses as in stop-motion animation. Again, the computer will work out the in-between positions. Because all of the objects are virtual rather than physical, there is much more freedom in motion. Physics and gravity need no longer apply, and lights and cameras can be moved around with ease. This freedom allows the motionographer to produce animated movement that could never otherwise be achieved in the real world.

Rendering

Once the animation has been set up satisfactorily it can be **rendered**. This is the process of creating each of the frames. A render can be set at different levels of quality. It is common to initially output a low-quality render first. This allows the designer to check that the animation, lighting, and framing is as expected. Because it is low quality, it renders reasonably quickly. Once everything is satisfactory, a final, high-quality render can be produced. The amount of time taken to produce the render will depend on the number of objects on screen, the number of polygons in each model, the number and type of each light, and the detail of any textures used. The time taken for a final rendered frame can vary from a few seconds to days.

Compositing

The final output render may be the end of the process if the finished film is purely CGI; however, a higher-quality result can be achieved by rendering out a series of different passes. This is particularly true if the CGI element is going to be combined or composited with some real-world elements. The different passes would normally include a *diffuse* or *beauty pass*. This is the basic scene without any reflections or shadows so that the colors are visible. This is then followed by things like a highlight or *specular* pass, a reflection pass, a shadow pass, an opacity pass, and an alpha pass. These individual passes are then composited together in a separate compositing software package, such as Adobe After Effects. The results are usually more fulsome than the basic render straight from the CGI software.

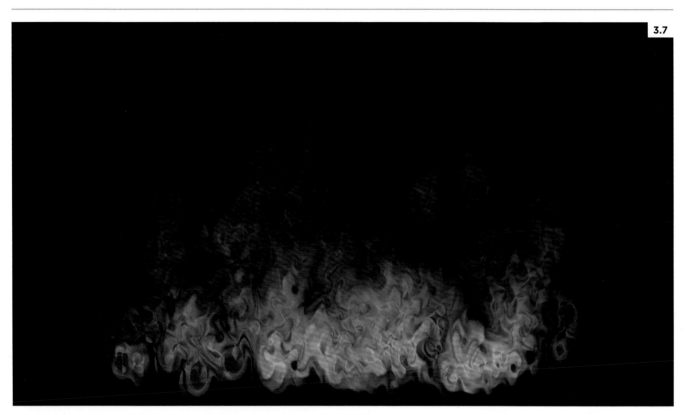

3.7

3.7 Procedural fire
Here the fire is created using procedural animation. The artist provides a set of criteria that describes how it will look and behave, but the actual animation is determined by the software.

TIP

PROCEDURAL

There is another method of animation often used in CGI that does not rely on the animator to control the movement. This is called *procedural animation*. This is where an object or series of objects are given a set of properties. These properties describe how the object would physically react and interact in the real world. They describe such things as elasticity, weight, and friction. The objects are given starting points in the first key-frame and then the computer works out how they would behave. For instance, a CGI ball could be given a material property of rubber and the virtual world could be given Earth-like gravity with minimal wind. The ball object could be placed at the top of a set of modeled stairs. The procedural animation would then calculate how the ball would bounce down the steps and move it accordingly.

Procedural animation is also used for simulations of things like cloth and liquids as well as atmospheric phenomena such as smoke and fire.

STEREOSCOPIC 3D

When we discussed three dimensions in the previous sections, we were talking about using the three axes of object placement, X, Y, and Z. This gives an illusion of depth and solidity, however the image is still on a flat plane. It is still ostensibly two dimensional. If we want to strengthen the illusion optically, we need to consider stereoscopy.

Because we have two eyes that are set slightly apart, our view of the world is always in three dimensions. Each eye sees a slightly different view of the world and our brain combines them to create a solid coherent vision. Stereoscopic 3D aims to reproduce this on the 2D plane of the screen.

Two images of the graphical scene, one slightly horizontally offset from the other, are viewed simultaneously. The larger the offset, the closer or farther away the object appears in the scene. When viewed through a device that allows each eye to only see one of the images, the result is a simulation of three dimensions.

3.8 Stereoscopic New York
In this example of a student film by Kim Langstroth, the filmmaker combines 2.5D animation with moving text and renders the output in anaglyph 3D to produce a fact guide to New York City. The red and blue images are slightly offset and composited over each other (bottom) to produce the effect of depth when viewed through red/blue glasses.

ASPECT
RATIO

DESCRIBING
OBJECTS
IN SPACE

2D
MOTION

2.5
DIMENSIONS

3D CGI

STEREOSCOPIC
3D

IMMERSIVE AND
AUGMENTED
ENVIRONMENTS

CASE STUDY:
MAKE
PRODUCTIONS

Different methods for viewing stereoscopic 3D

The first recorded 3D film was *The Power of Love*, shown in 1922. It used a system still often seen today known as *anaglyph*. This involved projecting the two images, one through a red filter and the other through a cyan filter. The viewer then watches the film wearing glasses with similarly colored lenses. The cyan lens cannot see the red image and the red lens cannot see the cyan image. Thus each eye sees its own image and the brain combines them to create the three-dimensional effect. While this is a cheap and easily distributable method, the results inevitably have a strange color cast.

An alternative is to use an active shutter system, often used in 3D TVs. In this system the two images are flashed on and off alternately and the glasses flash the left and right eyes on and off similarly. The problem with this system is that the glasses are expensive and can be cumbersome. There are also some cases where the flickering causes discomfort for the viewer.

A more common approach, often found in 3D cinema releases, is to use *polarized* lenses and to project the film through similarly polarized filters. The lenses are then only capable of seeing light that is of the same polarization. When the two images are projected together each eye will only receive one of the images, thus giving the 3D result. Polarized lenses give the cleanest and sharpest colors; however, special projection devices are required to use it.

Producing your own

Making 3D motion graphics is relatively simple. Most compositing software that is capable of using the X, Y, and Z axes to place objects and virtual cameras to frame the shots can be used. Any 3D modeling software would also be suitable.

The setting up of the scene is exactly the same as if you were going to produce a 2.5D or 3D image. Objects are placed on stage using Z-depth to place them at varying distances away from the camera. Any animation is then conducted as normal.

The difference, however, is that instead of using one virtual camera, you use two identical ones, offset from each other along the X axis. The distance apart is a source for experimentation.

The views from each camera need to be composited together into one scene. The camera on the left, however, is viewed through the *red channel* only, whereas the one on the right is viewed through the *green* and *blue channels*. When the two images are combined, the resulting image will have the typical offset red and cyan anaglyph halos.

The same technique can be also used to view on a 3D TV. Instead of using the color channels, the images are placed side by side on screen. The software within the TV will then interpret these two images into one three-dimensional image.

IMMERSIVE AND AUGMENTED ENVIRONMENTS

While not strictly a means of creating motion graphics itself, immersive and augmented environments provide a medium through which motion graphics can be projected. Commonly, motion graphics will be seen via a screen, whether that is on a TV or a monitor or via a handheld device or projected onto a surface. Immersive environments, however, aim to place the viewer inside the graphical display itself. The physical world is replaced by the virtual one. Augmented environments aim to place the graphical elements in the real physical world. The physical world is augmented or overlaid with extra information.

Defining virtual reality

Immersive and augmented environments can be described collectively as virtual reality. For a motion graphic to be considered virtual reality it must contain three main characteristics.

It must act as a *virtual world* where a viewer can exist and explore. As a result, it must exhibit three-dimensionality so that the illusion of reality is as close to real life as possible.

It must be *immersive*. This means that the viewer must either feel that he or she is physically within the virtual world or that the virtual world physically exists within his or her reality.

It must be *interactive*. That is, it must in some way react to the actions of the user giving them some form of sensory feedback. Typically, that means that the virtual objects will be able to be viewed in three dimensions by the viewers turning their heads or physically moving.

Immersive environments

An immersive environment is usually experienced through the use of some form of headset or glasses. The eyepieces transmit the images via tiny screens, each giving a slightly different offset view of the scene, producing the illusion of three dimensions.

The headwear will have movement sensors built in that detect the position and orientation of the viewer's head; this updates the view so the viewer is given the illusion of being able to look about the scene. The speed with which this updates is called *latency* (a lower latency corresponds to a faster update speed). Physical movement through the scene (e.g., walking) is usually produced through the use of some other input device (e.g., a game controller, mouse, or wand) rather than actually walking. Otherwise, the viewer is transported through the scene automatically.

3.9

3.9 Oculus Rift
The Oculus Rift offers an immersive method of experiencing digital content. Although it is relatively early in its development, there are already a number of content producers making materials for viewing immersively.

Augmented environments

Headsets come in several variations. The first and older version is the CAVE system (standing for Cave Automatic Virtual Environment). In this the users are placed in a room with the virtual environment projected on screens around them (and possibly above and below). The glasses convert the projected image into stereoscopic 3D while **tracking** the head position to update the visual display. Obviously these are very large physical spaces and not easily transportable. You probably would not have a CAVE system in your house.

A variation of the headset has a pair of tiny screens to project the stereoscopic images directly onto the viewer's eyes with motion sensors to, again, update the display. Until recently the technology was not really capable of producing a sharp enough image with a quick screen refresh to be convincing; however, advances in display screen miniaturization (led by mobile phone developers) has meant that this is now the preferred option. One of the leaders in this area is the Oculus Rift made by Oculus VR. This is a small, head-mounted device with incredibly sharp images and low latency leading to some very exciting developments in immersive environments.

An augmented environment does not require special headwear. Typically, an augmented environment means that the viewer looks at the real world through a screen upon which extra graphical data is overlaid. This gives the illusion that the virtual object somehow exists in the real world.

The most common way that this is experienced is through a mobile device like a tablet or a smart phone. Through a dedicated application, the camera is pointed at the world. The app then reads information from the device. This could be performed by using GPS compass and tilt data so that it knows where in the world, in what direction, and at what angle the device is pointing. Alternatively, the device recognizes a printed pattern within the image that corresponds with patterns in a database.

Once the app knows what the viewer is pointing the device at, it overlays the graphical imagery on top of the real image. This is then updated in real time so that the object reacts to the movements of the viewer.

Examples of wearable devices include the Google Glass project or the Oakley Airwave system. These devices project the overlaid information directly into the viewer's eye-line in much the same way as immersive environment headsets.

CASE STUDY:
MAKE PRODUCTIONS

Make Productions is an award-winning motion design studio based in London. It specializes in animation, visual effects, motion graphics, and creative online video content driven by design and narrative. In 2012, the studio won The Guardian Short Film Award. In 2013, its "Stand Up to Cancer" campaign (produced for Channel 4 in the United Kingdom) was awarded the bronze at the Bass Awards, which recognize broadcast design internationally. It also had a Vimeo Staff Pick for its short film *Lennon's Poster*.

Make was founded in 2006 by Joe Fellows, who studied at London's famous Chelsea and Camberwell College of Arts, where he also created short films and animated title sequences for the school, providing the foundation for his current work at Make. Over his career Fellows has also enjoyed directing and animating branding projects, title sequences, and station identifications for clients including UK Channel 4, BBC, H&M, and charities such as Shelter, Cancer Research, and United Way.

What software do you use and can you talk us through the production process of one of your parallax 2.5D sequences?
We mainly use AE but often supplement some elements with C4D. We often use Trapcode Particular to add dust and fine moving elements. We occasionally dip into our effect library for smoke and atmosphere.

Usually, we work from a still photograph, anything from historical archive photographs to glossy fashion shoots. First, in Photoshop, we cut out foreground and background objects and the main focus of the scene, such as a person dancing.

We study the photo and work out what the movement might be for both camera and subject, ready for when we come to animate. We then break up parts of the body into layers and retouch them, so it allows for greater latitude of movement when animating. We might cut out an arm and paint back up to the shoulder, so when we animate the arm stretching out, we can move beyond the boundaries of the original image.

We take the layered PSD into AE and assemble the scene. To add motion, we use a combination of puppet tool, distort tools, and a bunch of key-frames in the transform properties to manipulate the AE layers and bring the photos to life.

3.10

3.10
Joe Fellows of Make Productions.

3.11

3.11 _Cuba_—jumping boy
This sequence by Make is from a Kickstarter film for a book on Cuba. It shows how much motion can be achieved from a still image through the careful use of layers and image warping.

What is the key to a successful 2.5D sequence?

There are a few things I always tell my clients when embarking on a parallax project.

1. The animation is only ever as good as the original photo. If you have a poorly lit, badly composed photo, the animation will be poorly lit and badly composed.

2. It helps if the image is high resolution or at the very least HD screen resolution. When 4K (ultra-high definition) becomes the norm, the resolution will need to match its resolution or the picture will look "soft."

3. The best results come from an image that has depth with distinct foreground and background elements.

4. One of the most important things is that the original photograph captures movement, and I don't mean **motion blur** because that is not good. There needs to be innate movement within the subject of the photo, so for example, a dancing couple, a boy jumping, or an owl opening its wings in the snow.

5. No motion blur. Part of the appeal of the parallax animations is that they mimic super slow motion; you have very little motion blur on super slow motion footage.

You recently co-directed a shoot for an advertising campaign that uses your parallax animations. Tell us about that.

The shoot was incredibly liberating because we could set up the layers in real life. We were able to shoot clean back plates, capture specific foreground and background objects for set dressing, as well as isolate the main characters. The advertising campaign also required there to be a rack focus in the final commercial. This meant that everything had to be shot in focus so we could mimic the change in focus in post-production and create that cinematic depth of field.

What advice would you give on being briefed by a client?

In creative meetings, listen very carefully to what the client says and ask lots and lots of questions about the smallest details. The creative world is highly subjective and it's easy to misinterpret what someone is asking for. The question I ask most in meetings is "What do you mean by . . . ?"

Share lots of references. Other great work not only serves as inspiration and a talking point, but it's a useful opportunity to determine the scope and scale of the project, thus managing the client's expectations.

It's perfectly okay to push back. Adrian Shaughnessy summed it up perfectly: "Clients need to be challenged when they are wrong, and by not challenging them we are doing them a professional disservice." (*How To Be a Graphic Designer Without Losing Your Soul*, published 2005 by Laurence King Publishing Ltd).

How does Make Productions find work? Do you pitch or does work come to you?

We have a really solid client base in TV and regularly work with clients such as Channel 4 and the BBC. We also work directly with many big charities and have great relationships with agencies all over the world. At the moment we are working in London with Channel 4's *SomeOne* and we have just completed projects in Canada with [the public relations firm] TAXI and [for the film] *Strange Cargo* in Sweden. Make Productions has had some fantastic online recognition, which has opened up our client base globally and especially in the USA and Canada.

What type of projects do you want to work on more?

I'd like to work on more film title sequences. It's such a fantastic format and can be incredibly creative. I think this is partly due to the parameters you work within.

A title sequence can be highly conceptual or beautifully simple and [the complex] can be as rewarding as [the simple].

THE
CAMERA

DESCRIBING
OBJECTS
IN SPACE

2D
MOTION

2.5
DIMENSIONS

3D CGI

STEREOSCOPIC
3D

IMMERSIVE AND
AUGMENTED
ENVIRONMENTS

**CASE STUDY:
MAKE
PRODUCTIONS**

What was it that got you interested in working in motion graphics and what advice would you offer to someone starting out in motion graphics now?

These days the lines between motion graphics and visual effects or animation and compositing are wonderfully blurred and interwoven. When I was starting out in college I was doing stop frame, Flash animation, making puppets, short film, model making, sound design, and illustration. Today I am lucky enough to incorporate all of these skills into my work.

Don't just get inspiration from other motion graphics on Vimeo. Inspiration can be found anywhere. It's okay to ask if you don't understand. It's better to be sure of what you are doing than mess up a project because your ego got in the way.

Stay curious. Be polite. Be yourself. Take regular breaks!

www.makeproductions.co.uk

3.12

3.12 *Cuba*—laughing
Again, from the *Cuba* film, Fellows makes clever use of three dimensions to really create the illusion of depth. The way the building and chimney move, it is hard to believe that it is taken from a flat photograph.

This is complemented by a subtle use of rendered particle effects to add smoke and dust.

CHAPTER FOUR
CONCEPTS:
TIME

So far, we have considered the different types of elements that we may require: the digital cast members of our motion designs. We have also examined the importance of space, since one of the most important concepts of motion graphics is that these bits and pieces will move about.

We have seen how the two dimensions of height and width provide an arena for this movement to occur, and we have considered how the third dimension, the Z axis, is less tangible but nevertheless present as a territory to be utilized.

To fully chart the extent of our canvas, we need to introduce the parameter of *time*. Time is required for change to be apparent, and without change, we have no motion; our work would be little more than a poster or an intertitle. In this chapter, we consider how the invisible fourth dimension of time may be depicted and exploited in the creation of our moving images.

4.1 *Living Moments*
A special semicircular rig of 50 Nokia cameras
was created for this film by Paul Trillo. The images
captured were animated into a series of parabolic
portraits of life on the streets of New York City.

http://paultrillo.com

FRAMES

In Chapter One, we learned how a moving image sequence is a series of still images that are presented one after another. When we watch a movie, we never see these images at once; we see each of them for only a fraction of a second before it is replaced by another image. Each of these separate images in the sequence is known as a *frame*. Depending on the context, *frame* may describe a spatial phenomenon: the compositional space within the image boundary. In the current context of playback, the frame describes a unit of time: an instance in which the fluctuating arrangement of elements is observed or adjusted.

The timeline

Sometimes, the interface in which we view a completed movie contains playback controls and a timeline: a horizontal bar with a scrolling playback head to indicate the position of the current frame in relation to the full movie. The concept of a timeline is familiar to anybody who has used YouTube, but in many authoring environments, the timeline has even more importance.

In multimedia editing and compositing applications such as Flash, Premiere, After Effects, and 3DS Max, each frame of the movie sequence will have a corresponding **cell** or division on the authoring timeline. These divisions extend horizontally to represent the duration of the movie. Descending vertically down the timeline is a stack of layers, each one inhabited by various elements—video, vector shapes, type, CGI, mattes—that constitute the separately composited parts of the sequence.

Timelines are not the only method of depicting a motion sequence. Some multimedia programming environments, such as Adobe Authorware, present separate objects and their behaviors as an interconnected flowchart. However, the timeline is such an intuitive and ubiquitous metaphor for the invisible fourth dimension of a movie, it is inevitable that we will wish to fully exploit its potential.

Key-frames

The extended functionality of our timeline in multimedia software allows us to select individual frames or groups of frames and remove, add, or change their playback order. Crucially, the timeline also allows us to select and manipulate objects *within the frame* at a specific instance in time. If we wish to record a change to the attributes of one such element, we can record when this change should occur in a special kind of frame called a key-frame.

If, for example, we superimpose some red type into our movie, and we wish it to turn blue halfway through the movie, we can select the central frame of our timeline and promote it to a key-frame. With the key-frame selected, we can adjust the hue of our type. The single key-frame records the new default color state of the type, and it retains this for all subsequent frames.

Key-frames are the crucial sample points at which we can indicate how our design elements should change over time, and as such are one of the most important principles of motion graphics.

FRAME-RATE FRAME-BY-FRAME ANIMATION TWEENING STOP-MOTION TIME SLICE MOTION IN TIME AND SPACE EXERCISE: PLANNING AN ANIMATION

FRAMES

4.2 Key-frames

Put simply, key-frames indicate the moment at which change occurs in a sequence of images. The grid at the bottom of this illustration depicts a timeline of duration 25 frames. Key-frames appear in frames 1, 10, and 20. This is how the sequence would appear on playback: The movie begins with a red wedge, a blue cube, and a green cylinder on the stage. After 10 frames, the cube vanishes and after 20 frames, the cylinder vanishes also.

Key-frames can be used in conjunction with tweens in order to create less abrupt changes. For example, by tweening the opacity of the cube, we can make it fade away instead of disappearing.

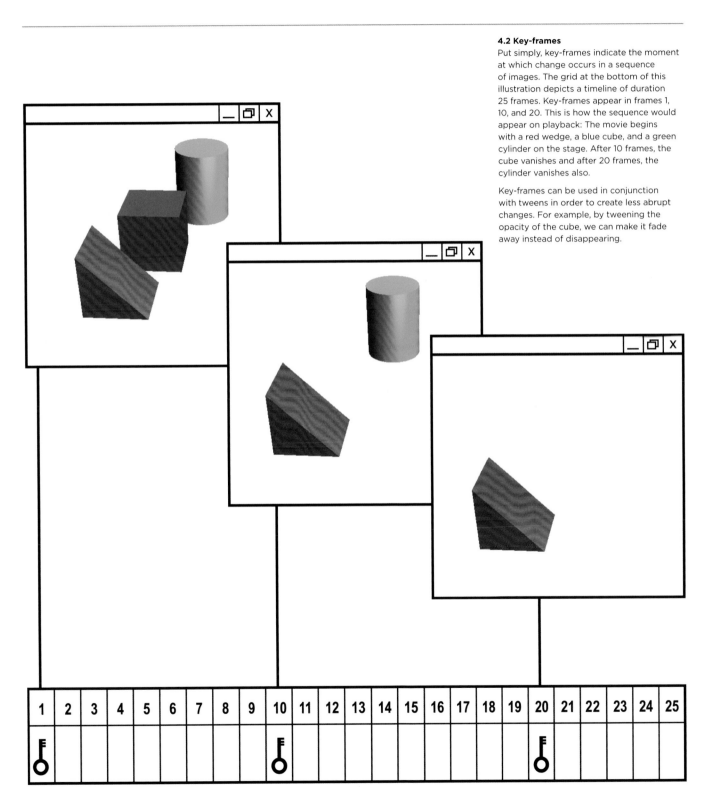

FRAME-RATE

All moving image sequences have duration. The duration of the movie is determined by two things: the number of individual frames and the frame-rate, the number of frames that are displayed during a set interval. We inherit the word *footage* from the origins of cinema; the duration of a film clip was proportional to the length of the celluloid strip, measured by the US standard foot. These days, it is more conventional to specify the duration of a video clip in minutes and seconds, and to define the frame-rate in frames-per-second (fps).

The duration and the frame-rate together reveal the number of component frames in a movie clip. A one-minute video of 25 frames per second contains 1 (minute) $\times$ 60 (seconds) $\times$ 25 (frames-per-second) equaling 1,500 individual frames of video.

Film and TV frame-rates are standardized. In the UK, the standard frame-rate for TV and video is 25 fps. In the US, the standard is 29.97 fps. Internationally, the standard frame-rate for film is 24 fps, although some film-makers have been experimenting with high-frame-rate (HFR) cinematography. Peter Jackson's *Hobbit* films were produced at double the standard frame-rate: 48 fps.

Animation and motion graphics that are created for other media platforms, such as the web, may have customized frame-rates. An animated GIF or Flash movie on a web page may possess a frame-rate of 1 fps, 10 fps, or 15 fps. With each frame there is new data to be delivered or computed. Too fast a frame-rate can result in too great a processing load on the target device; this can result in a delay while the image sequence is downloaded and reconstituted.

High-speed cameras

Frame-rate also describes the rate at which a camera records a moving image. Slow-motion cinematography involves shooting video footage at very high frame-rates—hundreds or thousands of frames per second—using specialized cameras. When this sequence is replayed at a conventional frame-rate, the effect is that time is dramatically slowed down. An event that lasts half a second in real time would take 10 seconds to watch back if shot at 500 fps.

This is not the same effect as slowing down footage, shot at a standard rate, using post-production techniques. In this case the software has to reinterpolate the frames to "guess" what would come between. The end result will be slower action, but the added frames will not be as sharp or accurate as footage shot on a high-speed camera.

FRAMES   FRAME-BY-FRAME ANIMATION   TWEENING   STOP-MOTION   TIME SLICE   MOTION IN TIME AND SPACE   EXERCISE: PLANNING AN ANIMATION

FRAME-RATE

Timelapse

As we have seen, frame-rate can be manipulated to produce a slow-motion effect. It can, however, also be manipulated the other way to speed things up. If we slowed the frame-rate down to one frame every second, a scene that we shoot over the course of an hour would result in 3,600 frames, or a little over two minutes at 24 fps. With this method, known as *timelapse*, we can capture motion that would not normally be visible. Timelapse is seen with scenes of fast-moving clouds or plants unfurling.

You can achieve this effect yourself by simply placing your camera on a solid surface and manually pressing the shutter release at scheduled intervals. However, you can achieve vastly superior results through the use of a tripod and an intervalometer, a device that can be set to automatically press the shutter release at timed intervals.

4.3 *Dance (RED) Save Lives*
Shots from a promotional video for a live-streamed concert organized to raise money for AIDS medicine in Africa. The footage, produced by Paul Trillo, was recorded at an accelerated frame-rate so that it can be viewed in slow motion, emphasizing the motion and energy of the performers.

The shower of pigment eventually settles to reveal the logo of the event: "(RED)."

http://paultrillo.com

FRAME-BY-FRAME ANIMATION

Frame-by-frame animation is the traditional animation technique. It has its roots in the nineteenth century with the advent of devices such as the *zoetrope*. It was developed much further in the early part of the twentieth century with the advent of the big animation houses. The process involves simply drawing each frame of the sequence on a separate page and then viewing the sequence in order at the desired speed.

The illusion of motion

The fact that we see moving images projected onto a screen or displayed on a monitor comes down to a quirk of human design. Rather than see an endless stream of individual images, our brain removes the pause in between and sees them as constant motion. This effect, known as the persistence of vision, is what enables us to create the illusion of motion through film and animation.

Planning the motion

Before an animator begins to draw, he or she will need to decide how many images per second are going to be produced. Full animation would use 24 images per second of motion; however, perfectly reasonable results can be achieved using half this. Anything much below this will result in the motion appearing jerky.

The animator then needs to assess the motion he or she is trying to recreate. Acting it out will give a good indication of how long a movement takes and hence how many images are needed. If a character raises his hand in half a second and the animation is going to be shot at 12 fps, then there will need to be six images in total.

A traditional animation process would then transfer this information to a **dope sheet** document that records the changes in motion over time.

4.4

4.4 Whiteboard animation
You do not need special equipment to create effective frame–by-frame animation. This sequence was created on a whiteboard. The camera is placed on a tripod in front of the board and the image is redrawn for every shot. The image sequence is then combined on a timeline to make the finished film.

Drawing the extremes

With the animation planned out, the animator will now draw the extremes of an action, that is, where it begins and where it ends. Once this is complete, they will draw an image that falls roughly halfway between the two end points. They will then repeat this process, adding images in between until they have completed the motion.

Onion skinning

Traditional animation would be drawn on thin paper over a **light box** in order to be able to see three or four images at a time. On a computer, the software will simulate the process through what is called *onion skinning*. This allows a number of frames to be visible at the same time, in the same position, but with varying degrees of opacity. The frame you are working on will be on top at full opacity.

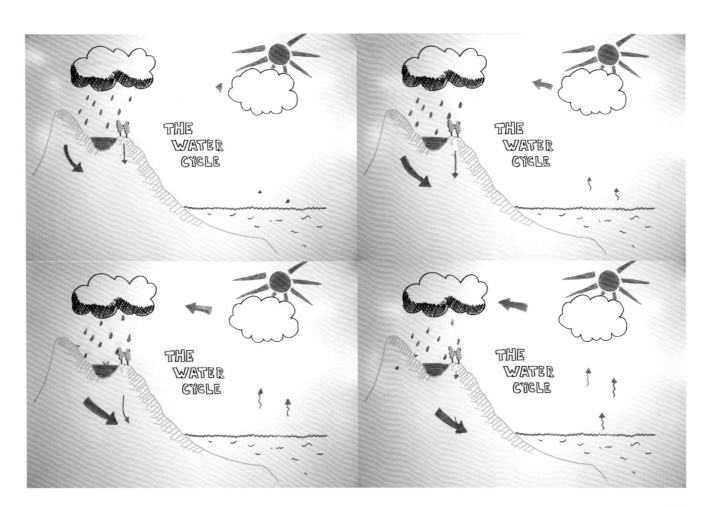

TWEENING

We have seen in the previous section that the traditional method of producing an animation is to draw each frame individually. This can be a long and laborious process. A five-minute film at 24 fps of full animation (i.e., one drawing per frame) would result in 7,200 individual drawings. This is a considerable amount of work.

Fortunately, with the advent of digital animation, we can now use a concept called *tweening* to help us animate objects in certain circumstances. The method is to create two images for the extreme ends of the motion required. These become the key-frames. The computer then automatically works out the stages in between and creates the intermediate frames.

Imagine, for example, you were creating the motion of a ball dropping from the top of the screen. Using tweening, you would draw the ball at the top of the screen, then draw the ball at the bottom of the screen. The tweening would then create all of the intermediate positions.

The beauty of tweening is that, because the intermediate positions are calculated by the computer, it is very easy to alter the speed. If you want the animation to happen faster, simply make the tween over fewer frames. If you want it to last longer, simply add more. If you want to change one of the positions, simply move the object and the tween will recalculate.

There are limitations, however. You could not use tweening to produce the full richness of movement in frame-by-frame animation. The two main uses are *motion* and *shape tweening*.

Motion tweening

A *motion tween* is the simplest. It calculates the change in physical properties of an object over time. In terms of 2D or 2.5D animation, this invariably involves a move along one of the X, Y, or Z axes. It can also, however, involve a change in orientation, rotation, size, color, etc. It does not alter the underlying structural shape of the object.

In the case of CGI animation this could be a movement of a limb on a character or the repositioning of an object in 3D space.

Often, multiple tweens are combined. An object might change position on screen while growing in size and altering its rotation, all at the same time. Usually tweens are chain-linked sequentially so that a series of complex movements and changes can be sequenced over time, building to a large range of movement.

Shape tweening

An alternative and perhaps less commonly used tween is the *shape tween*. In this case an object is created in one key-frame. On the next key-frame the shape of the object is altered structurally. This could involve drastically deforming the object in some way or could even involve creating an entirely new object. The shape tween then creates the in-between deformations, morphing from one shape to the next. In practice this can take some effort to work acceptably, and often, unpredictable results can occur.

| FRAMES | FRAME-RATE | FRAME-BY-FRAME ANIMATION | | STOP-MOTION | TIME SLICE | MOTION IN TIME AND SPACE | EXERCISE: PLANNING AN ANIMATION |

TWEENING

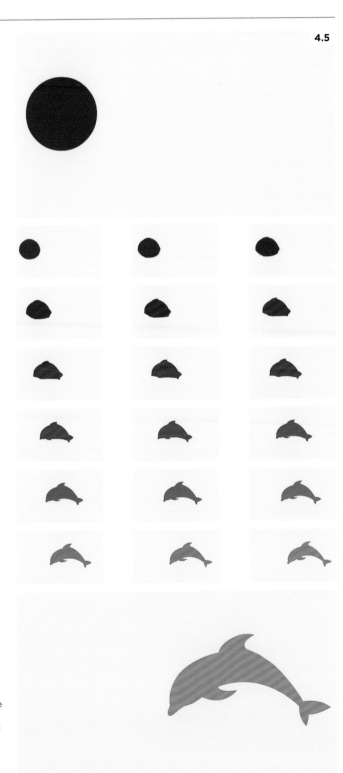

4.5

4.5 Shape tween

By declaring the start and end key-frames of an animation (top and bottom), we can entrust the computer software to estimate the appearance of the "in-between" images in a variety of ways. Here the circle progressively morphs into the shape of a dolphin. The computer software has determined what the in-between shapes should look like.

Please see www.bloomsbury.com/crook-motion-graphics for more on this project.

STOP-MOTION

Stop-motion animation is the process of photographing an object repeatedly, moving the object in small increments between each shot. This gives the illusion of continuous motion when the sequence is viewed back at speed. The origins of stop-motion animation are nearly as old as animation itself, with the earliest examples appearing in the late nineteenth century.

The technique, in essence, has changed little since its inception. The principles are still exactly the same. The earliest examples produced motion from inanimate objects such as toys. These simply moved position between frames. An early popular example of stop-motion are the films of Wladyslaw Starewicz of Poland, who in the early twentieth century created a series of films in which he animated dead insects that had been mounted on stands and rigged with wires to enable them to be repositioned. A simple wire skeleton can be created now, using materials such as florist's wire.

Armature puppets

A more robust version of wire figures is the armature puppet. Here a skeleton of metal bars joined by couplings that can be tightened enough to hold their position while being loose enough to move is built to form the shape of the character required. This is then covered with a skin, often made from latex rubber, that hides the underlying skeleton. This skin is then decorated with further coverings of hair or clothing, or is simply painted. This method enables the model maker to create highly detailed puppets with lifelike motion.

The motion is created by simply moving the puppet's joints a small amount at a time, photographing each position. Fundamentally, armatures have changed little from the earliest days when people like Willis O'Brien made *The Lost World* (1925), featuring stop-motion dinosaurs. Modern armatures, however, now contain intricate geared mechanisms that enable the animator to control things like facial features by turning threaded screws hidden in the figure's head.

Clay

A commonly animated material is modeling clay, whereby the animator manipulates a modeled clay figure between shots. This technique is sometimes known as *claymation*. The current masters of this technique in the UK are Aardman Animation, whose animated features and shorts have won awards around the world.

A clay figure, when subjected to the heat from set lights can, however, begin to soften and melt. It is common, when trying this technique for the first time, to look back at the results and see if the object has morphed its shape over time.

One way to counter this is to make a wire or metal armature skeleton first and then mold the modeling clay over it. This way the core shape of the object remains fixed. It also adds some rigidity to the puppet, enabling it to support its own weight better.

4.6

4.6 Brooklyn
In this short film to promote the Brooklyn Brewery MASH tour, Paul Trillo uses a version of stop-motion to capture a cyclist's journey through the district.

People and other objects

As we saw in Chapter One, stop-motion need not be limited to using carefully made puppets. Anything that is capable of being moved and of holding its position is suitable for stop-motion. Objects have included household items, food, sand, tea, tools, furniture, cars, and more.

Pixilation is a method, developed by Norman McLaren at the National Film Board of Canada, where the object to be animated is a human being. The person simply moves slightly between shots and holds still while the shot is taken. Using this method, highly unusual movement can be created where people appear to glide across the floor. If the person jumps in the air as each shot is taken, the resulting motion is that the person appears to be flying.

Another commonly stop-motioned object is a building block such as LEGO® bricks. There is a thriving community of animators that share their LEGO® films online at places such as www.brickfilm.com.

The trick with stop-motion is to consider anything a possible candidate for animating. Then you can begin to truly innovate.

TIME SLICE

Time slice is a special video technique for capturing and rendering moving objects in a live-action scene. The effect is a moving subject that appears to slow down or fully freeze in apparent defiance of the laws of physics. The effect that distinguishes time slice from a straightforward freeze-frame is that the camera orbits the subject, which stays in the frozen state.

The technique is decades old, but became a more conventional part of film language following the release of the *Matrix* films, in which a time slice technique (Warner Brothers dubbed their method "bullet-time") was used to depict actors suspended in mid-leap at the center of an arcing camera movement.

Early time slice methods involved the simultaneous exposure of an image over multiple cells of celluloid film. Artist Tim Macmillan devised a method that inspired the modern cinematic approach to time slice. In Macmillan's experiments, a length of 16mm film was curved around the subject inside the lining of a specially constructed camera the size and shape of a large wheel rim. Each cell of film had a corresponding pinhole in front of it, which was covered by a magnetic shutter; an electromagnet released all the shutters at once, resulting in the simultaneous capture of the subject from multiple, adjacent vantage points.

Since those early days, time slice technology has made many advances. These advances allow for multiple vantage points to be precisely aligned using laser targeting; for the images to be captured digitally on a spherical helix of cameras, as well as a band of cameras; for the images to be digitally processed and seamlessly combined; and for a timed interval to occur between the capture of images, resulting in hyper-slow motion instead of a fully frozen scene.

The challenges of time slice recording

There are several logistical challenges to time slice recording. First, the quantity of cameras required means that time slice is an expensive procedure. Second, the cameras must be securely mounted and precisely aligned around a subject. If each lens direction, distance, and focal length is not correct, then the image sequence will not be smooth. Third, the cameras must be precise, requiring a complex triggering system to be devised and installed. Finally, the extraction of the resulting images from the cameras and the subsequent processing and combination of these is very time-consuming.

Time slice is often combined with chroma-keying production methods (e.g., green-screen compositing) so that the cameras, which necessarily surround the subject and therefore appear in the background of most shots, can be removed and replaced with a more suitable background image. It has become a stunning but familiar element of the visual grammar of film and TV. It is often emulated in 3D software; an environment perfectly suited to the manipulation of vantage points within a three-dimensional space. Alternatives to time slice that create the same visual effect are achieved by mapping 2D images onto 3D models, or by the substitution of real actors with CGI counterparts.

FRAMES   FRAME-RATE   FRAME-
BY-FRAME
ANIMATION   TWEENING   STOP-MOTION   MOTION IN
TIME AND
SPACE   EXERCISE:
PLANNING AN
ANIMATION

TIME SLICE

4.7

4.7 Paul Trillo rig
Behind the scenes of the *Living Moments* film
seen on page 101. The arced rig was fully portable
in order to visit a variety of locations around the
city. The rig allowed for director Paul Trillo to
capture unique perspectives of New York City
and its inhabitants. Although this is a different
technique than the more conventional horizontal
time slice method, it shows how the inventive use
of cameras can create stunning effects.

MOTION IN TIME AND SPACE

When we move around in the real world, we feel multiple forces acting on and within our bodies. Even with our eyes closed, we can sense movement. In the digital domain, our perception of motion is constrained to what we can see and what we can hear.

The appearance of on-screen motion is relative. When all on-screen elements migrate across the frame at a consistent pace, this creates the illusion that the "camera" is the only moving object and that it is panning in the opposite direction. However, if one on-screen object is stationary relative to all other moving objects, this too may seem as if the camera is panning, this time tracking a single moving object.

Most of us are familiar with this effect from the classic *Looney Tunes* cartoons. A jet-propelled coyote may occupy a fixed pose at the center of a fixed frame. In contrast, the buttes of the Arizona skyline rapidly shift relative to his (and our) fixed position. The illusion is that the coyote—and our camera—are rocketing at high speed, even though it is the background that is animated. If the background was a starless night sky (i.e., a flat, solid color) there would be no frame of reference and therefore all parties would appear to be static.

Creating apparent motion therefore is a matter of contrast. We must consider which elements will move, and which will not, and what impression is created by the motion of multiple objects.

Easing

In the real world, objects do not move around at a constant speed. For example, a ball dropped on the ground will, upon bouncing, decelerate until it reaches the apex of its bounce as gravity overwhelms its upward energy, and then accelerate upon its return to the ground. Likewise, a pendulum will slow down as it reaches the extent of its swing, and travel fastest at the mid-swing point.

Motion graphics must be sensitive to the laws of physics if they are going to convince. This is why animated objects that disregard these laws—objects that move around at an invariable velocity—appear possessed of an intrinsic and disconcerting energy.

Newton's laws of motion describe how static objects are reluctant to move, and moving objects are reluctant to stop. Animation tools provide us with a technique to simulate these variable forces on objects. This technique is called *easing*. Easing is a conveniently applied property of a tween that automatically varies the velocity of an object according to its trajectory. With easing applied, an animated object will ease into a resting position, rather than halt abruptly and unexpectedly.

Motion blur

Movies are the illusion of movement: multiple photographs shown in a sequence, each one slightly different, to depict the progressive displacement of objects in space over time. We are all used to seeing this illusion on TV and in films, but one of the side effects of photographing a moving object in a series of still images is *motion blur*. The camera has an open shutter for a fraction of a second, but a fast-moving object in front of the lens will not halt obligingly during this photograph. It continues to move for the duration of the exposure, and as a result will appear blurred on each of the images in the sequence.

Motion blur is a technical shortcoming of camera technology, which is not evident in CGI-generated movies. This is because CGI does not *capture* multiple images; it *generates* and *renders* them. Motion blur does not occur.

However, we are so used to the phenomenon that it can be unsettling to see a moving image that lacks motion blur. For this reason, CGI animation often has fake motion blur selectively applied, to reinforce the illusion that artificial objects inhabit the same screen universe as live-action ones.

4.8

4.8 *The Zone*—motion blur

These images come from *The Zone* motion branding by Tendril. The sensation of movement and of speed is really heightened by the use of motion blur. The objects in the foreground are moving much faster in relation to the viewer and hence appear blurrier.

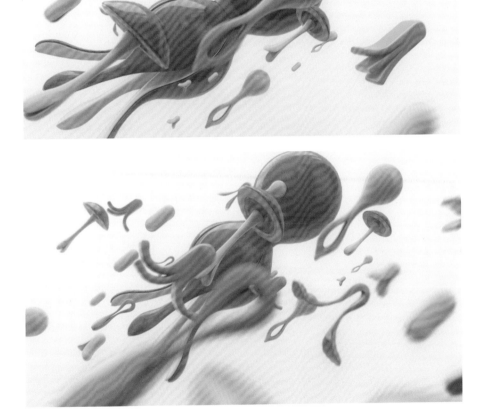

EXERCISE:
PLANNING AN ANIMATION

Summary

Before you begin to create a motion graphic piece you will need to accurately plan and record what you intend to do. This exercise will take you through the process up to the point where you are ready to begin animating.

Outcome

On completion of this exercise you will have planned a motion sequence for a TV title sequence.

Requirements

- stop watch
- pens
- sketchbook
- sticky notes
- lined paper

Step 1

Decide on a fictional TV program that you are going to design the titles for. At this point you only need a name and genre (e.g., *Cast Off* —a documentary about fishing).

Begin sketching some ideas for the sequence. Aim for 60–90 seconds. Use only text elements or simple shapes. Think about how the elements move and transition between each other.

Step 2

Transfer the main element positions (i.e., key-frames) on to sticky notes using words and images. This will allow you to add and change sequences until you are happy. Consider the flow of the whole piece as you build up your storyboard.

Once you are happy with the sequence, put the sticky notes onto some paper or a wall for reference.

4.9

4.9 Sketching ideas
Before you create any motion you need to capture your ideas and thoughts. Your sketches do not need to be works of art, but they do need to communicate your design.

Step 3

Now think about how long each element will take to animate. Use a stop watch to time them while visualizing the motion in your head. Note on the sticky notes the time taken for each.

On a piece of lined paper, draw a table that has a thin column on the left for the frame number, and a larger column on the right to describe the motion. This is known as a dope sheet (see 4.11).

Step 4

For this exercise you will be creating the animation at 12 fps. Draw a thick horizontal line every 12th row. Label the frame numbers in the left-hand column. You do not need to label every one; every 6th will be fine). Now look at the timings you worked out in step 3. Mark these on the sheet, remembering that 1 second = 12 rows.

In the right-hand column add a written description of the motion. You can write it on the line where an action begins and then draw an arrow down to where it ends.

Once you have transferred all of this information, you now have a sticky note *storyboard* and an accurate timing dope sheet to refer to when beginning your animation.

4.10 Storyboarding
Creating your storyboard on small pieces of paper or cards allow you to easily reorder them or make additions as necessary. For more on storyboards, see page 174.

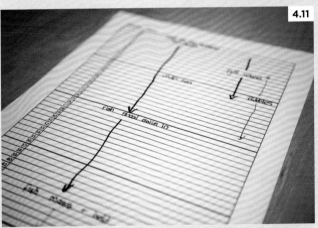

4.11 Recording the timing
The dope sheet is simply a record of the timings you intend for your film.

Please see www.bloomsbury.com/crook-motion-graphics for more on this project.

CHAPTER FIVE
PUTTING THE PIECES TOGETHER

So far, we have considered how the various design elements of a motion graphics sequence are arranged in space and manipulated over time. These two concepts alone are adequate ingredients for an animation sequence. But motion graphics can be much more complex than this; although effective motion design can be accomplished by the conventional animation of type and symbols, it will invariably require the addition of sound, at the very least.

Moreover, it is likely that multiple animated sequences, video clips, computer-generated imagery, and music tracks must be integrated to produce a cohesive moving image sequence. In this chapter, we look at some of the ways in which the various media components can be selectively and sensitively combined in post-production, and consider how this may impact the acquisition and creation of appropriate source material.

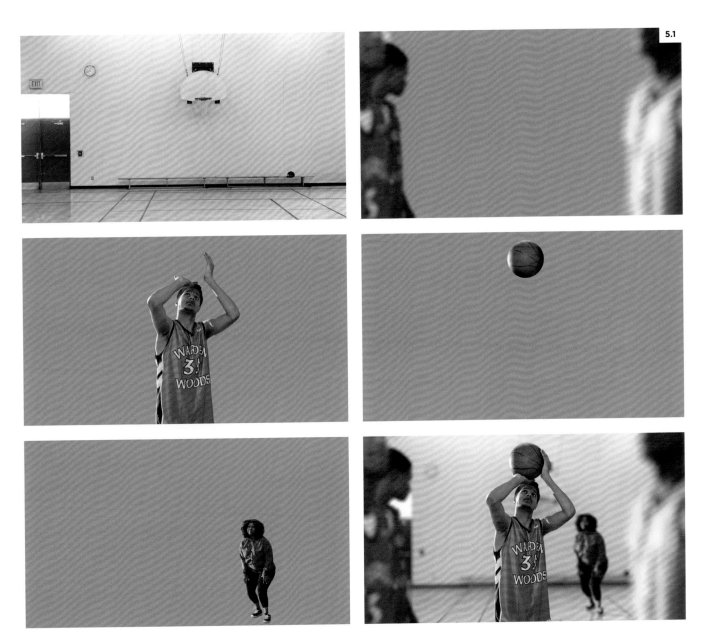

5.1 *United Way*
These are the component images of a TV
commercial for United Way by Joe Fellows of Make
Productions. The still images are masked, layered,
and subtly animated—figures are repositioned,
planes are scaled, and focus is selectively shifted
to create a hyperreal moving image.

www.makeproductions.co.uk

COMPOSITING

In most video-editing software, it is possible to layer video clips in a stack of coexistent video tracks. By default, when clips are layered, the top clip completely obscures the underlying video clips so that they are not visible. Although the associated audio of any underlying video clips may still be heard, the uppermost video track is the only one that will be seen in the end product.

By contrast to this straightforward layering of video clips, compositing is the overlaying and superimposition of two or more clips of video (or other image media) so that regions of all clips are visible within portions of the frame at the same time. For two clips to be composited there is an interaction between the pixels on each clip in the stack of layers. There are a finite number of ways that an uppermost clip can interact with a clip beneath it.

Transformation: The upper clip can be transformed by repositioning, rotation, scaling, or skewing. The remainder of the canvas will be empty, and the clip below will show through. A common term for scaling down a clip so that it covers a quarter or so of an underlying clip is *picture-in-picture*, or *P-in-P*.

Keying: This involves concealing part of a clip so that it is fully or partially transparent, and replacing this with something new. **Keying** involves the creation of a *matte* (the stencil used to delineate the mask parts of an image) and the use of a *fill* (the replacement of this hidden portion with an alternative image).

A simple way of keying a mask over a clip is to crop it. As the edges of an upper clip are dragged-in, a corresponding matte is created and applied; the layers underneath automatically inhabit the fill. A familiar result of this type of keyed mask is the *split-screen* effect, but more complex effects result from more complex types of keying, such as chroma-keying.

Transparency: The opacity of the uppermost clip can be reduced so that underlying clips are partially visible. The information regarding the transparency of clips is stored in parallel to the video color information, in a data component called the **alpha channel**.

Blending: The most complex and varied types of composites result from adjustments to the blending modes of stacked layers, alternatively known as *composite modes* or *layer-effects*. Blending modes involve mathematical comparison and combination of each pair of coincident pixels in the overlaid frames to produce an array of new pixels.

Complex composite video sequences may involve many, many layers of media interacting in different ways. Each one of these layers may itself be subject to other image adjustments, such as color or tonal adjustments. For this reason, authoring a composited video can become a challenging project that demands careful management of the media assets used, as well as a systematic plan as to how the neighboring layers of media should be arranged.

5.2 Dorset Cereal

In these two shots from an ad for Dorset Cereal by Nexus, the top image shows the shot as taken by the camera. Note the plain blue background that can easily be keyed out.

The lower image shows the shot as it finally appeared, with the blue background replaced by a nice morning glow. Note also that the rods holding the fox upright have been composited out by adding a copy of the empty background image over the top, thereby hiding them. In addition, limbs and eyes have been animated over the top using Adobe Flash.

www.nexusproductions.com

5.2

TRANSPARENCY

A full-color digital image or video clip is comprised of three color components called *channels*. These channels represent the separated quantities of red, green, and blue color components that are present in each pixel of the image or frame (see page 64). However, it is possible to include additional channels in a digital image file that do not relate to color information. Typically, we would use these additional channels to store information about transparency and opacity.

The additional channel used to store transparency information is called the *alpha channel*. Hence, full-color images that include alpha information are specified as **RGBA** images (red, green, blue, and alpha).

Most compositing software applications will allow the user, by means of a sliding scale, to adjust the opacity of a layer of video between 0 and 100 percent opaque. The value for the preferred transparency is stored by the software in an alpha channel. Transparency, like other clip attributes such as scale and position, can be key-framed and animated. Thus, a clip can appear to fade out steadily by tweening its opacity across only two timeline key-frames.

Layer opacity generally has an equal effect on all pixels; hence, a layer with opacity of 10 percent would render all sectors of the layer as virtually invisible. However, there are times when we wish selected pixels to be fully opaque and others to be rendered fully or partially transparent. For this, we would create a custom alpha channel that indicates the degree to which some sectors of the layer are transparent and others are not. To accomplish this, we fill the alpha channel with a matte.

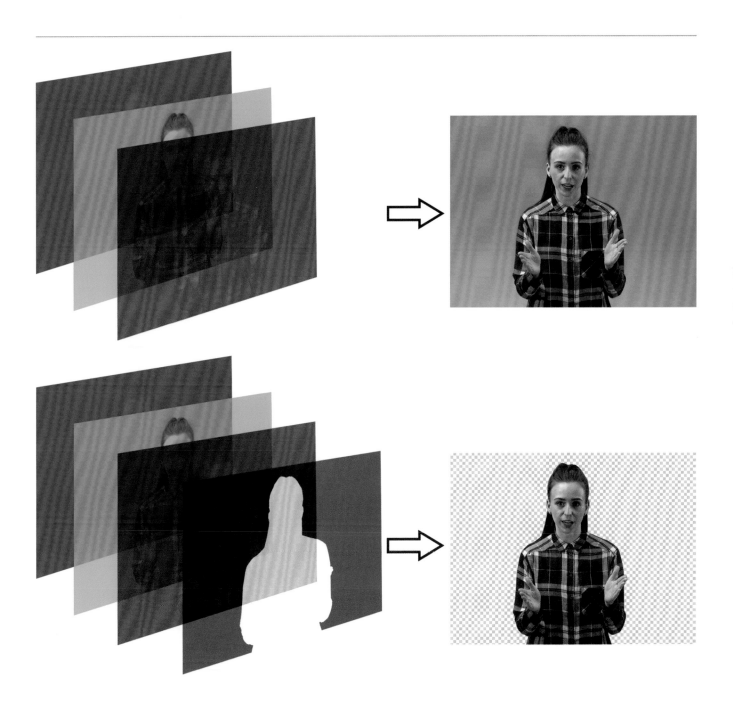

5.3 RGB and alpha
Most digital image files are comprised of three color channels: red, green, and blue (top). If we need to store information about which pixels should be visible and which should be hidden, then we can create an additional alpha channel containing a matte to indicate the transparency (bottom).

123

MATTES

A *matte* is an image reference that is used to indicate which parts of an accompanying video clip should be rendered wholly or partially invisible. Whereas alpha indicates the presence of transparency information, a matte is a specific "stencil" that resides *within* the alpha channel to control the variable transparency of different parts of the frame or image.

In the early days of cinema, a matte was a glass plate between the camera lens and the performers onto which a matte artist would directly apply black paint in order to prevent those areas of the film being exposed to light. In the digital era, a matte is a grayscale image or movie; the black parts of the matte signify the hidden parts of the video clip, the white parts correspond to those regions of the associated video that will be visible, any gray parts of the matte result in semi-opaque video footage.

A matte can be a static image. Alternatively, a *traveling matte* can be used: an animated movie clip of dynamic black, white, and intermediate gray areas. Any video sequence that has stark monochromatic content could be used as an effective matte: dark shadows or silhouettes against a white surface, black ink diffusing in clear water, or custom animations of shapes and patterns. These types of abstract mattes are seen everywhere, from title sequences to music videos.

It is common, however, for the matte to be an analog of the video sequence. For example, the matte will correspond precisely to the outline of a character or object within the frame.

Rotoscoping is one way to create a traveling matte that matches the on-screen activity. This is the frame-by-frame drawing of a contour to delineate the "seen" parts of the video from the "hidden" parts. Another method is to use chroma-keying: actors are recorded against a (typically) green background, and the post-production software produces a traveling matte based on the green pixels of each video frame.

Most title or image generation software is capable of automatically outputting a matte that corresponds to the type or objects that have been created.

Garbage mattes

Sometimes, the only parts of a video clip that we wish to conceal are those margins of the shot into which some of our production equipment or environment has intruded. For example, our green-screen stage, used for a chroma-key shoot, may reach beyond the extremities of our performers or props, but may not be quite large enough to entirely fill the frame of our viewfinder. Similarly, supports for lights, microphones, or models may encroach into the green-screen area. A garbage matte is a quick method of creating a boundary around our performers or props to eliminate these unwanted intrusions. A garbage matte is very coarse, and is always used in addition to a secondary, more refined matte.

Matte is a term used in the film industry where the discipline of hand-painting mattes originated. In TV multicamera environments, the terms *key* or *key signal* are synonymous with a matte. The matte is used in combination with one or two video clips. The matte selectively hides portions of one clip, and then "fills in" the gaps with the second video clip: this filling-in is known as *keying*.

5.4 Garbage mattes
A *garbage matte* is a commonly used matte in video compositing. Intrusive objects such as microphones (top) can be easily eliminated from a shot by creating a rudimentary "fence" that delineates the pieces of the shot to be excluded (bottom). This rudimentary matte can be used in conjunction with more sophisticated mattes such as chroma-key mattes.

Please see www.bloomsbury.com/crook-motion-graphics for more on this project.

COMPOSITING TRANSPARENCY

MATTES

KEYING

BLENDING
MODES

COLOR
ADJUSTMENT

SOUND

CASE STUDY:
MAX JAUGA

5.4

KEYING

Whereas a matte describes those portions of a frame that are hidden, keying is the name for the process of replacing this hidden area with substitute video material.

In order to key together two video signals into a composite video clip, three video components are needed: the *background* video; the *matte* (or *key signal*), which defines the region of the background video to be supplanted; and the *fill* video, which occupies the "hole" created by the matte. A matte, or key signal, can be rendered by post-production software.

Virtually all video-editing software has keying capabilities. In broadcast environments, the key is performed by digital video effects (DVE) hardware, such as a video-mixing desk in the studio gallery, or by means of keying software on a computer integrated into the video systems.

Methods of keying

There are several methods of keying. In the *preset pattern-* (or *shape-*) *keying* method of compositing two video clips, a key image (or matte) of a simple geometric shape is used to mask out part of the background image, and the corresponding portion of the fill image occupies this simple shape. The shape may have a feathered edge, or possibly an outlined (stroked) edge.

The *linear-keying* method is used when moving graphics are generated on the fly. The background image is generated by a CGI workstation with video output capabilities, and as the rendered image animates, a corresponding key signal is generated that is inverse to the composed shapes and text. Linear keying is used in real-time situations where there is no opportunity for post-production, such as live sports or news coverage.

When the background video signal is shot to include a region of a specific luminance (brightness), we can use the *luma-keying* approach. The video-editing software or hardware can dynamically generate a key signal using a high-contrast video, for example, a dark silhouette recorded against a bright background. The bright background could be designated as the key value, so a key signal that matched this bright region is created; the fill signal replaces the bright background of the video image. Alternatively, the darker silhouette of the background image could be nominated as the key luma value, and the silhouette would be replaced with the fill video.

Chroma-keying

Probably the most well-known method of keying is chroma-keying, also referred to as *green-screen* or (less widely) as color separation overlay (CSO).

It works on a similar principle to luma-keying; the difference here is that a specific color hue is used to generate the key rather than a dedicated brightness value. Typically, green and blue are used as the key color due to their scarcity in skin tones, but in practice, any exclusive color could be used to derive a chroma-key signal (or matte).

Typically, an actor is shot performing against a vibrant backdrop. Successful chroma-keying relies upon a clear distinction between the actor and the backdrop, in which there is no elision between the hues of the foreground actor and the hues of the backdrop.

Occasionally, inconsistent lighting on the backdrop can result in an inconsistent spectrum of hues and tones across the backdrop. This can make it difficult for the keying software to distinguish an accurate matte. Also, reflected light may cast a slight green hue onto the actor; the result is that affected portions of the actor may be keyed out along with the backdrop.

Chroma-keying has become an increasingly accessible technique. Even established digital media agencies will make creative use of quite modest green-screen equipment for the purposes of compositing.

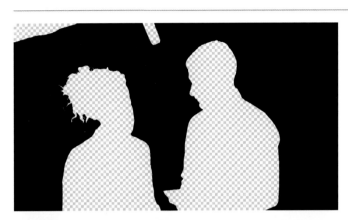
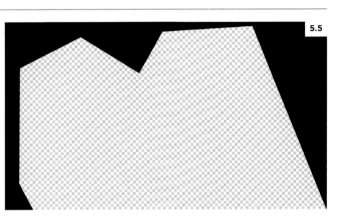

5.5

5.5 Chroma-keying

A moving matte is created by referring to and masking out the green pixels of each frame (top left). A garbage matte (top right) is applied in order to eliminate stray objects that were recorded in front of the green backdrop (center left). The original footage combines with the moving matte and the garbage matte to create the semi-transparent footage (center right). A background fill image (bottom left) is then superimposed into the transparent footage in order to create the final composite (bottom right).

Please see www.bloomsbury.com/crook-motion-graphics for more on this project.

127

5.6

5.6 *Heroes and Generals*
Behind the scenes of a shoot for the trailer
for Reto-Moto's *Heroes and Generals* game.
Actors perform in front of a green background,
sometimes suspended by wires. The computer-
generated battleground, explosions, and artillery
were composited around them in post-production.

www.territorystudio.com

COMPOSITING TRANSPARENCY MATTES

KEYING

BLENDING
MODES

COLOR
ADJUSTMENT SOUND

CASE STUDY:
MAX JAUGA

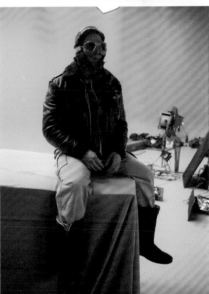

BLENDING MODES

We have learned how one method of compositing two video clips is to place one on top of the other and add a *blending mode*. Blending modes take the name of the different mathematical interactions that can be applied for a composited pixel to be generated from two source pixels. *Add*, *subtract*, *divide*, and *difference* are examples of blending modes that are unambiguously mathematical. Fortunately for us, the compositing software takes care of the complex math. It is important for us to understand the science, however, so that we can faithfully select the most appropriate blending mode in a given situation.

The arithmetic of blending modes

For the sake of simplicity, let's consider a frame of a video clip that is made entirely of blue pixels. Above this clip, we will overlay another frame of video that contains black-and-white stripes. What would the resulting, composited video frame look like if we set the blending mode of the uppermost clip to, say, "multiply"? In multiply mode, the numerical value of each upper pixel is multiplied by the value of the pixel on the layer below it to produce the value for the new, composited pixel.

In our scenario of black-and-white stripes above a blue background, each of the black pixels has a value of zero, that is, minimum brightness present across all three RGB color components. When the black stripes blend with the blue image beneath it, the emergent pixels will have a value of the blue value multiplied by zero, equaling *zero*. Hence, the blue pixels are reduced to blackness where the black (zero-value) pixels are overlaid.

A white pixel has a pixel value of 100 percent (maximum brightness) for each of the three color components. Therefore, when the white pixels blend with the blue beneath them, the resulting color is 100 percent blue. The original blue value is unchanged in the composited result, leaving a final composite of black and blue stripes.

There are many different types of blends that can occur, but at their heart is straightforward arithmetic, like the multiplication above, conducted simultaneously on partnered pixels. We can categorize blending modes based on the likely outcome of the blend.

5.7

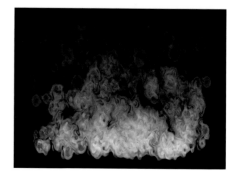

5.7 Two images, multiple blends
These two images of a synthetic flame and a vectored dolphin can be superimposed using a variety of blending modes to create different composite images.

Categories of blending modes

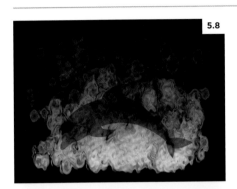

5.8

A composite that uses *multiply* blending mode will never produce colors that are lighter than the components. This is also the case for other subtractive modes such as *darken* or *burn*.

Additive blending modes will result in brighter composite colors. *Add*, *lighten*, *dodge*, and *screen* are examples of these. Care should be taken with additive blends as the resulting value may exceed the maximum brightness permitted. The consequence is that some regions of the video image may "clip," appearing burned-out.

Complex blending modes such as *difference*, *soft light*, and *hard light*, will create lighter or darker images depending on the source values, and may have different results if the stacking order of the layers is changed.

Naturally, many millions of mathematical calculations are conducted in an instant: for each pixel of each frame of video, and for each layer of video. Considering that each frame of video contains over two million pixels, the liberal compositing of clips can be taxing on the computer hardware and software. For some compositing software, it is impossible to compute and display new video information at a speed required for steady playback. In these situations, the video must first be *rendered* (at a slower-than-playback speed). It can then be viewed or exported at a normal frame-rate.

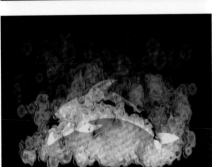

5.8 Blending results
Some of the results of blending the two preceding images of the flame and the dolphin. From top to bottom: multiply, divide, subtract, and difference blending modes.

COLOR ADJUSTMENT

When we combine elements together they inevitably bring attributes with them (e.g., size, position, rotation, texture, shape). We can alter and modify all of these to produce a coherent composition. One attribute, however, that does not affect the composition, but does have a drastic impact on the overall look and feel of the piece, is the color. Each object or layer will have its own color data, possibly carefully designed to work well in itself. However, when the elements are combined, the way the colors work together becomes important.

The process of conforming colors within your piece and particularly between shots is known as *color adjustment*. This enables you to ensure that all of the sections you create are harmonious and feel like part of one whole. Imagine you are overlaying a set of images on top of some previously shot footage. The colors of your overlaid graphics should match elements from your underlying footage. The purpose of this adjustment is purely to tie the separate elements together.

Most post-production or compositing software and much image-editing software has some sort of color correction facility. Often this consists of a set of color wheels allowing you to pull each of the colors (red, green, and blue) in the desired direction. Sometimes rather than red, green, and blue, the adjustment wheels are for shadows, mid-tones, and highlights, but the concept is the same.

5.9 *THE SHELL*—color

In *THE SHELL*, by Momoco, there is a distinct color theme across the whole film. The palette is made up of warm browns and greens accented with cold blue and white highlights. This accentuates the theme of the story of a city trapped under a giant organic shell. The color becomes an integral part of the visuals.

www.momoco.co.uk

Color grading

Another step that is commonly considered after adjustment is **color grading**. Technically the process is the same as adjustment, using the color wheels, but rather than attempting to unify the elements and provide harmony, the aim is to provide an overall color theme.

This allows you to define how your piece feels. If you want it to feel like a vintage piece, you might give everything a slightly sepia tone. If you want something to feel like it was part of surveillance footage, you might give it a desaturated green tone.

You might create a whole set of elements in full color, but then decide that the overall look should be black and white. Using color grading techniques, you can alter the colors and tonality to reduce the saturation, giving it a rich black and white.

Grading your piece is not essential but it is a useful and convenient tool to make simple but drastic changes to the look and feel of your whole piece.

SOUND

Regrettably, sound is often a neglected dimension of motion-graphic design. Inadequate planning and poor production values in the audio department can undermine the most sophisticated of visual sequences.

On occasion, the full soundtrack of a motion graphic will be delivered as a fixed and unalterable foundation of a client brief. Lyric music videos, for example, are an "illustration" of an existing music track; the sound is serviced by the motion graphics. Similarly, a vocal track, such as a lecture or product explanation, may be the basis of and justification for a motion-graphic sequence.

For other projects, we may be called upon to influence, to design, or even to produce the sound as well as the moving images.

Sync sound

Sync (synchronous) *sound* is audio that has been recorded at the same time as the video images, such as the voices of actors in a scene with dialogue, or a presented **piece-to-camera**. Although most camcorders have professional microphone inputs, the sync sound will often be recorded onto a separate audio recorder; a clapperboard provides a common visible and audible reference that allows the discrete recordings (video and audio) to be realigned at the editing stage.

The best way to capture usable sync sound is to record in an acoustically suitable environment designed to limit unwanted reverberation or extraneous sound. In addition, the microphones must be placed as closely as possible to the source of the required sound.

However, at times, it is impractical to record impeccably clear sync sound. Your actors may be competing with traffic, wind machines, or poor acoustics. They may also be framed such that closely placed microphones would be visible in the shot. In these situations, the sound may be re-recorded in post-production.

5.10 *Strike Suit Zero*
In these images from the game *Strike Suit Zero*, motionographers Territory produced HUD overlays as well as cinematics and a trailer. The very nature of the material means that there is no existing sound. Everything heard has to be generated from scratch. The sounds and the visuals need to work perfectly together, each complementing the other.

www.territorystudio.com

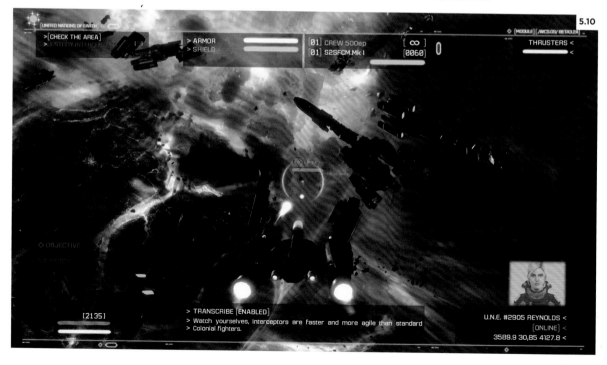

ADR and Foley

Automatic dialogue replacement (**ADR**) is the re-recording of performance dialogue after the performance was originally recorded. The actors may have originally performed in a noisy environment, or in circumstances that prevented the close placement of microphones. Under the controlled environment of a sound recording booth, the actors are asked to review their performance and, as they watch, to replicate the cadence and rhythms of their original vocal performance, often line by line, until the re-recording is natural and convincing.

Foley is another post-production process for creating audio for film and video. A Foley artist will make use of conventional audio tools—as well as household items and specially constructed contraptions—to ingeniously recreate noises for on-screen activity. Foley can be used to reproduce naturally occurring sounds seen within the frame, or to fabricate sounds for objects that do not exist outside of the digitally created screen universe.

The motion graphics we create will often be entirely fabricated in the digital realm. But in order to create the illusion that the objects on the screen have real-world attributes such as mass, speed, and texture, we must capture, create, and combine sound from various sources. In truth, nobody knows what a Tyrannosaurus rex sounded like, but your viewers will be disappointed and distracted if it is silent. Similarly, a gigantic, metallic font emerging from a ball of flames will be expected to exhibit an equally bombastic sound.

CASE STUDY:
MAX JAUGA

Max Jauga, freelance compositor and 3D generalist, claims to have become a VFX junkie back in 2003 when he rendered his first teapot and learned what an alpha channel was. For the past five years, having worked professionally with a vast array of agencies, studios, and individuals and on a variety of projects, he feels he has built a solid understanding of VFX and 3D production.

His on-set experience has also helped him to understand production needs and budgets. His passion is compositing; however, he freely admits to getting his hands dirty with 3D Studio Max or Maya to do some general 3D work. He is also happy working with code and will write small Python scripts in order to optimize his production workflow. He always enjoys cracking a technical challenge.

What was it that got you interested in visual effects?

I used to play a lot of video games when I was a teenager and once the game was done I used to love doing customizations with the built-in editors. It got to the point where I started looking into how I could potentially put my own models into the game—that's when I got interested in 3D. Then I saw the *Killer Bean* video by Jeff Lew and decided that I wanted to do something similar. I remember rendering an alien for one competition and my computer (800mgz Pentium IV with 64 Mb of RAM) couldn't handle more geometry than I already had in the scene. So I decided to experiment and put the rendered model into a photograph. To do that I had to learn the compositing side of things and when I blended those two images together I was really amazed how much you can improve your CG render with the help of post-production. And so the compositing was the next thing that I wanted to explore. Until this day it's something that I enjoy the most—compositing CG and live action together.

What would a typical workday be like for you?

It really depends on what type of project I'm working on and where I'm working. If it's a post-production house I usually start my day with checking tasks on a tracking software (for example Shotgun or Ftrack) and then getting on with the tasks. If I have submitted any shots the day before I might have a review session at the screening where my work will be reviewed by supervisors and/or clients and I will get feedback.

If I'm working from my office then it's usually email and render checks in the morning and then tasks that I need to go through the day. I might need to call or Skype with a client in order to discuss the progress of a project or to clarify something.

5.11

5.11 CGI and compositing
In this still from one of his films, Jauga has
expertly composited a CGI character that he
built and animated seamlessly into the video
sequence. Through the use of motion tracking,
matting, and effective lighting, the realism and
believability is maintained.

How is working for yourself different from working for an employer and what made you go freelance?
Going freelance happened very quickly. The post-house that I was working for at the time ran into financial difficulties and the company had to be liquidated. There were a few unfinished projects and I continued working on them. Then I got introduced to a few people who were looking for freelance artists and it all started from there.

When working for yourself you definitely have more responsibilities. It's on you to do your finances, tax returns, business development, etc. You have to wear a lot of different hats in order to have everything running smoothly.

A lot of people say that it's freedom that attracts them to freelancing and while that's true to some extent, there are definitely a few "gotchas." The nature of post-production these days means that a lot of things need to happen quickly and if you're off for a while it can be a deal breaker.

However, freelancing can be very rewarding. You're not locked into one job so if you want to make more money you can always take on another project. You can arrange your day how you want it. If it works for you, there is no reason why you can't start your day at 11 a.m. rather than 9.

For me the big plus when it comes to freelancing is the ability to choose your projects. If you feel that you don't like the project or you want to work on something else—it's your call.

How do you find your work?
For studio work I usually just email the post-house with my show reel. I'll check the company's webpage to see whether they are looking for people with my skills. If so, I'll contact the recruiter.

Most of my freelance projects come from recommendations or people that I worked with before.

5.12 Render passes
In order to fully composite the CGI elements into the finished filmed scenes, Jauga renders several different "passes" of each element, allowing the blending of them to be selectively superimposed upon each other at a later stage.

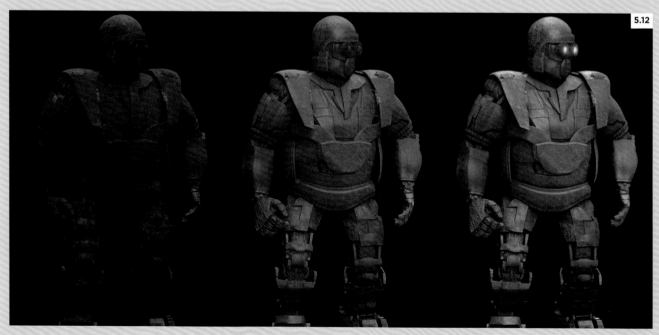

5.12

5.13

Which of your jobs has been the most challenging and why?

There have been a lot of challenging jobs. The one that comes to my mind is the *Talking Cows* TV commercial that I had to work on at the very early stage in my career. The idea was to film real cows and then replace their mouths with lip-synced CG mouths. There were a lot of challenges on that job, from cows not really wanting to cooperate on-set and licking off all the tracking markers to various technical issues that we had to overcome while working to a very tight deadline.

Do you think that your degree was instrumental in getting to where you are now?

I definitely improved and gained a lot of new skills while I was at university. At the same time, a degree on its own (at least in a VFX field) won't get you a job. You need to have strong skills that you can use in production and demonstrate them in your show reel.

It's hard to say whether I could have learned as much by teaching myself. I think university gave me a chance to try out different things that I would probably otherwise not have had a chance to experience. However nowadays there are newer things out there for you to learn and quite a few alternative ways to gain new skills.

www.maximusworks.com

5.13 CGI modeling
Jauga was initially self-taught in CGI modeling, lighting, and animation, skills that he now uses successfully in his career as a freelancer.

CHAPTER SIX
RECORDING AND RECREATING MOTION

Most of the preceding chapters have concentrated on some form of mark making, digital or otherwise. The motion that is created is generated by the user, often within the computer through the manipulation of objects over time and through space. These movements can be planned meticulously, with pixel precision, to ensure that the object moves exactly how and where we want.

However, in the real world, things move more chaotically. There are no end of small factors (e.g., wind, surface properties, gravity) that affect the motion of an object. Sometimes it is desirable to emulate this real-world motion with all of its inherent variances to produce a more believable result.

This section will study the use of natural, real-world motion itself as a means of generating the animated motion. This can be done through rotoscoping, motion tracking, match moving, and motion capture (all of which capture different elements of a performance), or by simply introducing a virtual camera that can produce framing and motion similar to ones we are used to seeing.

6.1 Facial motion capture
This facial motion capture rig from Vicon allows
for the accurate capture of the movement of
the face. The two infrared cameras mounted
on the arms in front record the position of the
reflective dots applied to the actor's face. This
data is captured in the software and can then be
applied to a CGI model, providing highly lifelike
movement.

ROTOSCOPING

Rotoscoping is a technique, which comes from animation and VFX, which can help reproduce a realistic motion. At its most basic level, rotoscoping is simply tracing. An action is filmed and the resulting sequence is projected one frame at a time. Each frame is then traced by a rotoscope artist using whatever drawing method is desired. Each traced frame is stored as an individual image.

The resulting images are then recomposited back together to form a new sequence, producing a drawn or illustrated motion that closely matches the original filmed material.

The technique is used to either reproduce a highly natural motion in an animated object or to separate a filmed subject from the background for recompositing into a new sequence. Either way, the core process is the same.

6.2

6.2 Rotoscoping a dancer
The dancer is first filmed against a plain background. Each frame of the clip is then manually traced to produce the paper cutout-style behind the figure of the final sequence.

Please see www.bloomsbury.com/crook-motion-graphics for more on this project.

MOTION
TRACKING

MATCH
MOVING

MOTION OR
PERFORMANCE
CAPTURE

EXERCISE:
ROTOSCOPING

ROTOSCOPING

History

The rotoscoping process was conceived and developed in the early twentieth century by the animator Max Fleischer in his film *Out of the Inkwell* (1915), which featured a rotoscoped dancing clown. He patented a rotoscope system in 1917, which consisted of a projector that produced an image one frame at a time onto the back of a piece of frosted glass. The animator would place his or her paper onto registration pegs on the glass and trace the projected image, thus producing the rotoscoped animation.

In subsequent years it was used in numerous films either as the sole animation technique or as one part of a larger sequence. The underlying principle changed very little.

The biggest change came in the mid-1990s when digital techniques became possible. MIT computer scientist and animator Robert Sabiston developed a system of computer-assisted interpolated rotoscoping, called Rotoshop, that automated much of the process. This was used extensively by director Richard Linklater in his films *Waking Life* (2001) and *A Scanner Darkly* (2006). The Rotoshop software is proprietary, but that and similar processes have since been used in many films.

Animation

Using rotoscoping for animation produces a highly realistic looking motion, irrespective of the mark-making technique employed. Early examples simply took the motion and used it as it was, without further manipulation. The first feature-length Chinese animated film, *Princess Iron Fan* (1941), was almost exclusively rotoscoped. Many Russian films from the 1940s and '50s featured rotoscoped animation in an attempt to impose a style of Socialist realism that forced many more artistically experimental animators out.

Later, rotoscoping was used as a guide to a more stylized look, as in the video for the band a-ha's song "Take On Me" (1985), which combined live action with a sketchy pencil style.

More recently it has been used extensively in the marketing for Apple's iPod, with the now widely familiar dancing silhouettes.

VFX

Within the discipline of VFX, rotoscoping is used primarily to create moving masks over filmed material. This is often used in object removal, where an object appears on screen that the director does not want in a shot.

A "clean plate," a shot without the object, is acquired. The rotoscoper then goes over the original footage, drawing a mask over the offending object. The mask is then altered frame by frame to produce an animation.

The rotoscoped mask is then used to hide the object and let the clean plate show through. This is often used for rig removal, for example, hiding equipment used to support an actor in a shot.

Rotoscoping is often the entry-level role in the VFX industry.

MOTION TRACKING

Imagine watching a video of a person walking across the screen from left to right. Now imagine placing your finger on the screen on the head of the person. Follow the person's head with your finger as the video plays and they walk. Now imagine the path that your finger has just traced across the screen. This is a track of the motion of the person's head.

Motion tracking, then, is the automated process of following an object on-screen in a previously filmed piece of footage to create a virtual track. The position and time data of that track can then be applied to another object, giving the impression that the new object is attached to the original object.

In the example above, imagine that we track the person's head. Then we could composite a hat to the video footage using the track data and the person would appear to be wearing it.

6.3

6.3 Motion tracking

Here, Adobe After Effects has been used to track the position of the corners of a card held by the actor. The use of two track points allows for any rotational motion to be captured.

Once the positional data has been analyzed it can be applied to another object, in this case a card design.

Please see www.bloomsbury.com/crook-motion-graphics for more on this project.

Tracking an object

Most video post-production software has some form of motion tracking. The actual process may vary slightly from application to application but the basic concepts are the same.

First you need to find something suitable in your footage to track. The ideal is a smallish area of relatively high contrast. Since the application is essentially dumb, it cannot recognize an object for what it is. Instead, it uses pattern recognition to find an area of pixels. As a result the pattern needs to be easily identifiable, relatively unique, and not likely to change much over the duration of the clip.

Once a suitable area is identified, a track point is placed over it. This is simply a rectangle that defines the pattern that the software will look for and the area around it that it will search in. If the subject is fast moving, and consequently the pattern will move a larger distance between frames, then the search area will need to be larger than if it is slower moving.

If we are doing a simple track to record the motion on the X and Y axes, one track point is fine. If, however, our subject contains some rotation, then we need another track point. The process above is repeated so that we have two points on either side of the object. The software will now be able to analyze the position of each point in relation to the other and then work out what rotation is required.

Analyzing the motion and reapplying it

Once the track point or points have been set, the software will automatically analyze the footage. It will move forward or backward one frame at a time, searching for the pattern and moving the track point accordingly. In most cases this is automatic; however, occasionally the process needs to be halted and the track points realigned manually. This will be a result of the pattern being momentarily unrecognizable due to things such as motion blur or something passing in front of it.

Once the analysis is complete, you should have a line drawn on the footage with a series of points on it. The line represents the path described by the object over time and the points represent the frames.

This set of tracking data can then simply be applied to the new object. The data contains information on the frame number and X and Y coordinates for each. This data, when applied to the object, will cause it to move on screen in direct relation to the original footage.

Motion tracking and motion graphics

This process will be used in one of two ways: either to make a new object follow a filmed subject as if it was attached to the subject, or to add a new object into the background of some moving camera footage so that it appears to be fixed into the scene.

Examples of this are often seen in news infographics. A news presenter will do a report from an outside location. When the presenter wants to give some illustrative information the camera will pan slightly to one side, revealing a suitable space where the animated infographic will appear fixed into the filmed world alongside the presenter.

An alternative that is commonly seen is when subjects appear on-screen and we want the viewer to see some information about them. The information can appear to float beside them, following their movement on screen and thereby confirming their relation to the information.

Motion tracking is an ideal way to embed extra visual information into a scene, but it will only work in two dimensions. We only analyze the X and Y coordinate data. For motion that is more complex and that requires Z axis data, we need to consider *match moving*.

MATCH MOVING

As we have seen in the previous section on motion tracking, it is possible to analyze a previously filmed scene to extract motion data in order to use the data to composite a new object into the scene. This is fine as long as the original camera movement is only confined to the X and Y axes. The analysis only works in two dimensions and so anything added to the scene will inherently be two dimensional.

What if the camera were moving through a scene? Inevitably there will be three-dimensional movement. Objects that were not visible at the start of the scene may become visible as the camera moves. In this case a motion track will not give us the required results. This is where we must use match moving.

There are many examples of software that is designed to undertake match moving. Two of the most common ones are Vicon's Boujou and Imagineer Systems' Mocha, which both produce three-dimensional data to be used in other software. Other software, such as Blender and Adobe's After Effects produce 3D data and can also be used to composite the final visuals.

Solving a scene

The first step in producing a match move is to track points, using the same principle as in motion tracking. A point of contrast is identified and then followed frame by frame. The difference here is that the software automatically identifies a large number of possible points and tracks them over the duration of the filmed scene. These points can be altered manually if needed.

Once this is complete, the data could be used as 2D tracking information for a motion track. What sets this apart is that it can also be analyzed to produce a 3D *camera solve*. In other words, the relation between each point is analyzed and from this analysis the position and motion of the original camera is deduced. Information such as lens type will make this process smoother and more accurate. Using the deduced information, a virtual camera is created that exactly mimics the position and motion of the original camera.

A **point cloud** is also created. This is a collection of dots that represent the position of the objects in the scene in 3D space.

Compositing content into a scene

The "solved" 3D point cloud is then imported into software capable of 3D CGI. This will create a scene that has the same number of frames as the original footage at the same frame-rate. A virtual camera is created that mimics the original camera and the points are then visible, giving an impression of the filmed scene. Using the data, a *ground plane* is determined that indicates where the floor in the original footage would have been.

Using all of this data, 3D objects can then be created and positioned in the scene. The motion of the camera around the object will give the illusion that the CGI object is locked to the original scene. Lighting must be created within the CGI program that mimics the original lighting of the filmed scene as closely as possible.

A number of versions, or "passes," will usually be produced in order to create the base render, mask pass, lighting, shadow passes, and so forth.

These are then composited together on top of the original footage, completing the illusion that the 3D CGI object is part of the originally filmed scene.

Uses for match moving

Match moving is used extensively in VFX, with most shots requiring some sort of match moving to enable a convincing composite of the digital elements with the real ones.

This is often used in documentary-type programs, particularly of a historical nature, where extra visual data is composited into a filmed scene to demonstrate how a scene filmed today may have looked in the past.

The work involved in producing a highly successful match move is quite considerable, potentially utilizing multiple pieces of software and a variety of different skills. It is worth asking whether a full 3D solution is really essential or whether, with a little lateral thinking, a simpler 2D motion track could suffice.

6.4 Match moving

In this example, Adobe After Effects has been used to capture some movement data. After analyzing and solving the footage, the software produces small, colored points that correspond to areas of the frame. When the footage is played, these points follow the objects they are attached to.

They can then be used as the basis for positional data for compositing other objects into the scene, for example a sign on the wall in the background.

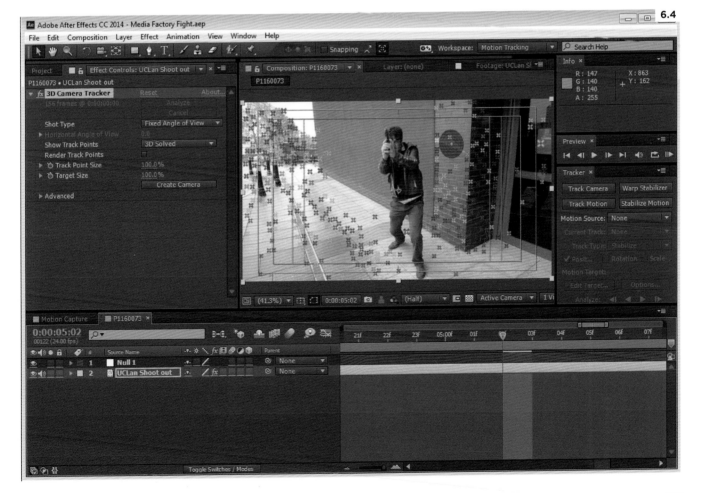

6.4

MOTION OR PERFORMANCE CAPTURE

Performance or motion capture (sometimes referred to as *mocap*) is not to be confused with motion tracking or match moving. Where they rely on previously filmed footage to extrapolate positional and motion data, motion capture derives its data directly from the live performance.

Through the use of specific data-capture technology, an actor's performance can be accurately recorded and then applied to a new 3D CGI actor and replayed over and over from different viewpoints. This is the technique that has been popularized by the actor Andy Serkis and his company The Imaginarium Studios through his work in *The Lord of the Rings* (2001–2003), *King Kong* (2005), *Rise of the Planet of the Apes* (2011), and other films.

The equipment needed for motion capture is highly specialized and expensive and, as a result, out of the scope of most amateurs. There are, however, an increasing number of production houses that offer the service on a project-by-project basis, thereby doing away with the need to purchase expensive equipment and facilities.

Capturing the performance

Most motion capture is performed using a marker system. The basic setup consists of a series of cameras positioned around a large performance area in which an actor performs wearing a suit with highly reflective markers at each joint.

The cameras are unconventional in that the lens is surrounded by a ring of infrared lights that project out onto the scene with the camera able to pick up any infrared light that bounces back from the reflective markers. The exact number of cameras required varies, but at the minimum there should be at least three cameras able to see each marker at any given time.

The cameras feed their data back to software that interprets the signals by triangulation to recreate a 3D set of points that directly mimic the position and motion of the points on the performer. After undertaking a short calibration test in which the performer stands vertically with arms outstretched (in what is known as the *T stance*), the performance can take place without the worry of being framed correctly in the shot.

What is recorded is the set of point data, rather than visual image data.

Applying the data

Once the point data is recorded, it can then be matched to a 3D CGI model. The model is rigged so that it has a similar structure to the points recorded from the performer. Each point is then assigned to a corresponding position on the model.

Once the model is rigged with the points, the recorded movement data is applied. The result is that the CGI figure will replicate the movement of the performer. The number of markers and cameras used will affect the quality of the capture.

Once the basic performance has been applied to the CG figure, an animator can then go back through and finesse any movements, as well as position the virtual camera wherever desired.

The virtual set

Rather than recording an actor's performance, an alternative approach to motion capture is reproducing camera moves. A virtual set must first be created using CGI. The motion capture artist then uses a T-shaped stick with reflectors at each end, rather than a full body suit. The stick is moved around in the recording space and the movement and position is translated into movement and position in the virtual set.

This way a director or camera operator can try a number of camera movements before deciding on the best one. This also opens up the possibility of reshooting material after the actors have left.

Use in motion graphics

Motion capture is primarily used in character animation and as such is utilized extensively by the film and game industries. It is also often used in the realms of medical and sport science to accurately record a person's movement. It is here that the discipline of motion graphics can play a part by way of communicating the information to the viewer.

Virtual sets are another commonly seen example, as many programs, particularly for news and "magazine" shows, are actually recorded on green or blue screens. The set seen by the viewer is created entirely by software, and the movement of the cameras around it are controlled using virtual camera motion-capture techniques. The presenters are then composited onto the virtual set and the background is chroma-keyed out.

6.5

6.5 Capturing motion
To capture realistic movement, a motion capture rig is required. The performer wears a figure-hugging suit covered in highly reflective balls. The movement of each ball is then tracked by a set of infrared cameras and the position data is then triangulated to create a digital recording of the performance.

EXERCISE: ROTOSCOPING

Summary

Rotoscoping is sometimes thought of as a cheating way to animate, as the motion is first filmed and the animation created by tracing over the video sequence. However, this is short sighted. With a bit of planning and some creativity, great results can be achieved that cannot really be achieved any other way.

Outcome

On completion of this exercise you will have created a short rotoscoped sequence in a visual style of your choice.

Requirements

- a video camera
- software to convert the video into an image sequence and back (As well as the major motion-graphic software mentioned elsewhere in this book, there are many freely available programs and apps that will automate the process for you.)
- a printer
- paper
- drawing or mark-making tools
- a scanner or camera
- video-editing software

Step 1

Using your video camera, record some motion. This could be a subject moving or it could be you moving the camera within a static scene. To make it easier for yourself, ensure that the subject is clearly delineated from its surroundings. If you are filming a person, film them against as plain a background as you can. This will help you identify the subject when you get to the rotoscoping section.

Step 2

Generate a series of still images and save them in a folder on your computer.

If your video camera records and outputs an image sequence, use that setting.

If your video camera only records and outputs video formats, use an online video converter to transform it into a series of stills.

Step 3

Print each frame/image onto a separate piece of paper. Quality is not a real issue here as long as you can see the image clearly. Be warned that if you film at 24 fps and your clip is 10 seconds long, that is 240 individual images. You might choose to print only every other one. This will drastically reduce the amount of printing as well as the amount of tracing work. Set your printer to add the file name to the bottom of each image so that you can keep the images in the correct order.

6.6

6.6 Print your frames
When you print out your frames, ensure they are large enough to see the object you are going to trace and that they contain the numbers of the sequence.

Please see www.bloomsbury.com/crook-motion-graphics for more on this project.

THE
CAMERA

MOTION
TRACKING

MATCH
MOVING

MOTION OR
PERFORMANCE
CAPTURE

**EXERCISE:
ROTOSCOPING**

6.7

Step 4

You now need to trace each image onto a new piece of paper. The choice of drawing style you use is entirely up to you and will provide the style of the finished result. Remember that you do not have to draw the whole image. You only need to draw the area of motion that you want to rotoscope.

Remember to write the number of the image in the sequence at the bottom of each page. It will be more difficult than you may imagine to reassemble them in the correct order without page numbers.

Step 5

Once you have completed all the images, scan or photograph each one back into the computer. Again, ensure that you use a sequential file naming system (e.g., MyFile001, MyFile002). This will ensure that the sequence remains in order within the folder.

Using the video-editing software of your choice, import the image sequence as footage.

You will now have a rotoscoped video. You could use it as it stands. You could also composite back over the original footage to incorporate the video and drawn elements together.

6.7 Trace the images
Use a thin tracing paper so that you can easily see the image below that you are tracing. Alternatively, use a light source to shine through.

6.8 Finished rotoscope
The style you use for your rotoscoped sequence is entirely up to you.

6.8

CHAPTER SEVEN
PROCESS: PLANNING

It could be argued that the most important point in any motion graphic project, indeed in any design project, is the time *before* you begin to make the product. This is the time when you will be formulating your ideas. You will be working out what may or may not work without the expense or time of actually producing anything. In a commercial world, this is very important and could potentially prove very costly if not approached thoroughly.

To enable this idea-generation exercise to be as rich as it might, it is important that you develop the mindset of a designer. This will involve constantly being on the lookout for ideas and inspiration to draw from when a project requires it. This is a series of habits that you can easily learn to cultivate, but you need to actively pursue them in the first place.

Similarly, once you are into the designing and creating process, there are a number of practices that you can develop to make this aspect run smoothly. In this chapter we will be looking at the areas of a motion graphics project that will enable you to plan properly. We will look at some practices you can indulge in to develop your general creative thinking. We will then look at some techniques and methods that will make the planning process as efficient as possible.

7.1 Wash design

Wash is a digital design agency from the north of England. Its studio is used as a creative space where ideas are generated and shared, enabling the entire team to have input.

One wall is a large chalkboard so that team members can scrawl ideas as they come up with them. Others are covered with work in progress.

They surround themselves with inspirational work and ephemera to help the creative process.

www.wash-design.co.uk

MESSAGE AND AUDIENCE

Although motion graphics requires creativity, ingenuity, and skill, we must remember that it is not fine art. Motion graphics is more akin to graphic design, which is known alternatively as *commercial art*. Motion graphics is, therefore, concerned with selling, promoting, explaining, or informing. Our mission is to ensure that effective communication takes precedence over artistic expression. Hopefully, there will be room for both, but if the motion graphic does not convey the required information, then any artistic qualities are futile.

By developing a habit of sketching or otherwise gathering inspiration, we are primed to selectively synthesize a variety of visual influences into a rich and original response. But too immediate or intuitive a response to a design problem is not appropriate. We must resist any impulsive or radical ideas and attempt to be much more tactical to be sure that the purpose of the motion graphic is considered. Our mission is to analyze the problem at hand, systematically devise alternative solutions, and evaluate how appropriate these solutions are in relation to the parameters of the problem and the intended audience.

Analytical thinking

Analysis is the process of breaking something down into smaller pieces in order to get a better understanding of it. Analytical thinking is a highly regarded skill, and is a necessary early step in the design process. Analysis is often facilitated by using a framework to organize our observations and ideas about a problem. The SWOT framework (strengths, weaknesses, opportunities, and threats) is a familiar structure to assist with a systematic analysis, but other analytical frameworks can be adopted or created.

Theoretical models of communication can provide us with alternatives to the generic SWOT framework. One such model is the SMCR (source-message-channel-receiver) model of communication, devised by David Berlo. We can use his categories to organize our initial thoughts about what and who our motion graphic is for and how it may be subject to interference or misinterpretation.

If we regard our motion graphic creation as the message then we, the designers, are the *source* of the message according to Berlo's model. Although there are other factors that determine the success or failure of a motion graphic to communicate, the source has a tremendous influence.

This influence may be negative or positive, so an analytical approach may help to identify any intrinsic potential for miscommunication. Conscious reflection may help us recognize the extent to which our beliefs, values, and experiences will influence—and potentially taint—our design ideas. For example, we can ask ourselves: What are our core motives for creating this message? How do we hope the work will change or impact upon the viewer? What secondary motives may be acting upon our thinking? Do we possess any assumptions or lack any knowledge or cultural awareness that could taint the message?

7.2 Analytical frameworks
Models of communication, such as David Berlo's SMCR model, provide us with useful frameworks to analyze what our motion graphics must do and who they are for.

7.2

By considering the *message*, we can consider the actual content of the motion graphic. The message incorporates image, type, and color with intimate associations; employs design principles to create emphasis and structure; and has duration and dimension.

There are many, many decisions about the message to be made at the design stage. Which media will be included? Will we make use of video, sound, music, and/or type? How will these elements be combined and arranged? Which brand values will be emphasized? What intertextual or cultural references will be made by our choices about typography, color, language, and the "human elements" (e.g., class, age, gender, ethnicity)? What do all theses aspects *mean*?

The *channel* can be regarded as the medium or platform through which our motion graphic will be viewed or distributed. The channel impacts the size, the technical quality, and the context in which the message is experienced. As a result, the channel dictates the *fidelity* of the message, so we must ask ourselves how the channel could disrupt, degrade, or subvert the message. Will the channel be a gigantic screen? A tiny screen? One of multiple, competing animations, ads, or pop-ups? Will the viewing context be the home, the cinema, the office, or the bustle of an airport departure lounge?

The *receiver* is the "decoder" of the message; in our context, this is synonymous with the viewer or audience. The success with which our communicative intentions are conveyed will depend on the literacy, knowledge, attitude, and values of the receiver. If we make invalid assumptions about these, the viewer may be resistant to our message or confused by it. Will they be able to decipher our ornate typefaces? Will the colors, personalities, sounds, and typefaces create adverse **connotations** in their minds?

The most useful attribute that we can adopt in considering the needs of the receiver is *empathy*. By placing ourselves in the shoes of the viewer or viewers, we can attempt to answer significant questions that should influence our designs: What are their expectations? How conservative or progressive are their tastes? How disparate or uniform are the individuals in the audience? Are we addressing schoolchildren or their grandparents?

An insight into the audience does not arrive by brainstorming; knowledge and understanding of the audience arises from research and observation. Target users may even provide feedback on early prototypes to help refine design thinking and improve design solutions.

User research, analysis, and iterative design may seem like an obstacle to the creative activities of media production. However, these steps are necessary if we are going to create motion graphics that do more than just look cool and actually address a meaningful need for our clients, as well as their customers or users.

SKETCHBOOKS

What it looks like

If you are initiated into an arts discipline or program of study, you have probably already been indoctrinated into the habit of maintaining a sketchbook. A sketchbook can be a welcome companion in a coffee shop, a waiting room, or on a long journey, as it enables us to record ideas and observations as they occur to us that would otherwise be fleeting.

You may regard your sketchbook as a conversation with your future self; alternatively, you can think of it as an extension to your visual memory and imagination: a place to deposit your ideas, no matter how purposeless or unformed. At a future date, when your creative energies are depleted, your sketchbook may provide the starting point from which a focused design solution emerges.

It is equally conceivable that you use your sketchbook not as an archive or "idea bank," but as a creative playground or gym. Just as dancers might prepare for a performance with a regime of stretching out ligaments and flexing muscles to encourage the flow of blood and oxygen around their limbs, so too can we prepare for our work by stretching and flexing our creative muscles. A sketchbook is a suitable venue for this.

The goal of keeping and regularly using a sketchbook is not to labor toward an immaculate volume of exquisite artwork. Similarly, the marks made need not serve as a blueprint for a larger work in progress. Sketching is concerned with the process as much as, if not more than, the end product. A sketchbook is a tool to facilitate our visual curiosity and playfulness. By keeping and using a sketchbook, we can remain alert to the novelty and variety of visual culture. Our actual drawing capabilities are less important than the regular habit of observing and exploring.

Sketchbooks can take many forms. You may use them as a point for collecting work by other designers whom you find inspiring. Alternatively, you may use them as a way to collect somewhat mundane visual material that could serve as a creative trigger for solving visual problems. Scrapbooks may be filled with newspaper or magazine cuttings along with accumulated ephemera such as tickets, flyers, or images. You might collect appealing swatches of color or intriguing combinations of typefaces.

Sketchbooks are not the purview of fine artists or designers working in two dimensions alone. Graphic designers, typographers, sculptors, filmmakers, and animators have found sketchbooks to be essential to their practice.

MESSAGE AND
AUDIENCE

SKETCHBOOKS

COLLECTING
INSPIRATION

THE DESIGN
PROCESS

THE
PRODUCTION
PIPELINE

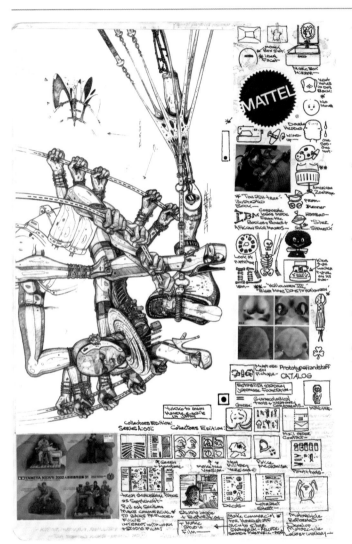

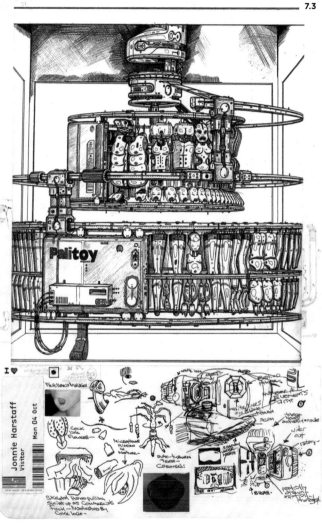

7.3 Sketching motion

Johnny Hardstaff is a director, designer, and modern storyteller who has created work for Twentieth Century Fox, Xbox, Sony, Radiohead, and the BBC. He is also a prolific sketcher.

His sketchbooks often feature storyboards for recording and exploring time-based ideas. In addition, Hardstaff collects ephemera such as magazine cuttings and stickers. These are often arranged in patterns and rhythms to capture or provoke ideas about motion and change, even on the static page.

www.johnnyhardstaff.com

COLLECTING INSPIRATION

Digital tools

To be creative means to generate something that was not there before, and to create something wonderful requires craft, effort, and imagination. But directing effort at our craft skills alone will not allow us to create anything truly original. We must also direct energy at improving our ingenuity, and a good way to accomplish this is to be more alert to those things around us that inspire, motivate, and impress us. By establishing and maintaining a habit of observing, recording, and reflecting, we develop a reservoir of experiences, observations, and inspirations. These are the fuel—the raw materials—of our creative responses, and they can be found in a variety of places.

Smartphones and the World Wide Web have provided us with innumerable digital tools to assist with our creative habits. With the immediacy of the Internet, we can instantly find thousands if not millions of inspirational images, videos, and tutorials.

Social bookmarking tools like Pinterest or Tumblr are a potential depository of inspirational imagery.

There are several web-based magazines that showcase exceptional design and professional works in progress, such as formfiftyfive.com, behance.net, and dribbble.com.

As well as uploading or searching for images on hosting sites such as Flickr, tiny video clips can also be created and shared using smartphones in conjunction with apps such as Vine. Many video-bloggers have demonstrated that the six-second limit of uploads can accommodate original and novel visual ideas.

Digital productivity tools can be very enabling and supportive, helping to structure and capture our ideas. But we must also acknowledge that the digital universe is home to innumerable distractions. So at times, we may arrive at more original ideas by ditching the tablet or smartphone and looking farther afield for creative stimulation.

MESSAGE AND
AUDIENCE   SKETCHBOOKS   **COLLECTING
                            INSPIRATION**   THE DESIGN
                                            PROCESS   THE
                                                          PRODUCTION
                                                          PIPELINE

7.4

7.4 Inspiration

These pages from the notebooks of Paul Greer, a CGI artist working in Bristol, UK, demonstrate how anything can act as an inspiration, from scenes to quotes.

burningfp.com

Travel

One of the best ways to challenge our own assumptions about how things should be, look, or sound is to travel beyond familiar territories.

Exploring an unfamiliar foreign city can be an assault on the senses. We may not understand the language on the street signs and shop fronts, but this allows us to consider the visual arrangement of the imagery and letterforms without the obstruction of their implicit meaning.

Perhaps a little globetrotting is not within everyone's budget, but guidebooks, magazines, street-view online maps, and even learning a new language can substitute for some of the first-hand enrichment of travel.

Get cultured

Since ancient times, narrative art has been sewn into tapestries, carved into stone pillars, and painted onto cave walls. Complex graphical information has been depicted in maps, charts, and diagrams for centuries. Our current conventions of modern typography began with the phonetic alphabet during the fifth century BC.

If we look beyond Western civilization, other cultures have their own heritage of language, writing, and visual communication. We should expose ourselves to as much of this as possible; otherwise, our own work may appear to be a mere pastiche of our own popular-culture references.

Beyond the visual arts

Music, in all its forms and genres, can provide tremendous inspiration. Listening to a short piece of unfamiliar music and letting your visual imagination wander may prove more productive than hours of aimless Googling.

Inspiration is everywhere; in nature there is an abundance of growth, change, movement, and transformation. Architecture, sculpture, and fashion are sophisticated fields that, like motion graphics, are concerned with space and dimension, and sometimes movement. Dance is another art form with a long heritage that explores movement, time, and space. Theater and puppetry are similar. Sports reveal how the human body can occupy a space or a period of time. A visit to a zoo, a park, a ballet, or a basketball game may provide as much visual inspiration as a trip to a museum or art gallery.

It would be very short sighted for a contemporary practitioner of motion graphics to draw inspiration only from the relatively recent era of digital animation and visual effects. Our responses to motion graphics are influenced by our immersion in an established and evolving visual culture that extends back to prehistoric times. We should embrace this rich legacy and fully exploit it in our own work.

MESSAGE AND
AUDIENCE   SKETCHBOOKS   **COLLECTING
                              INSPIRATION**   THE DESIGN
                                                  PROCESS   THE
                                                                   PRODUCTION
                                                                   PIPELINE

7.5

7.5 Journey notes
While on a very long train journey Paul Greer drew
the horizon as it presented itself—a constantly
renewing subject that changed at a rate that
could be captured on the page. The lower half was
drawn on the return journey by car when at rest in
parking lots.

THE DESIGN PROCESS

A simple Internet search will reveal a plethora of variations of the design process. Some are specific to an individual discipline, others may be particularly vague. However, there is a general consensus across them all that the process contains three general steps: planning, designing, and refining.

The design process should be cyclical. That is, it begins at a point, moves from stage to stage, and eventually returns to a variation of the start point where it begins again. A particular piece of work may go through many **iterations** of the design process or it may just go through once, but it needs to visit each stage to inform the next.

A project will start with an objective. This may be a self-set project, something you have chosen to do purely for yourself. More likely it will be something someone has asked you to do. It may be an assignment for a course. It may be a commercial piece for a client. Either way, you need to understand the objective and be clear on what is expected of you.

It is a common error at this point to turn on your computer, start up the software of your choice, and begin creating. This misses out some of the key points of the design process and will in all likelihood result in a weaker end result.

Planning

The planning stage is probably the most important and possibly the one that gets missed most often. This is the point where you must clearly define what is required. The objective may be deliberately open, giving you the freedom to be creative, but there will be constraints. Ask yourself where the work is to be seen, who the audience is, and what the message is that you aim to convey. Think about any specific requirements that may be needed.

Once the objective is understood, it is time to begin the idea generation through brainstorming, mood boards, research, and so forth. (See previous sections in this chapter for ideas on gathering inspiration.)

Planning can then take the form of writing an idea treatment and script, and developing storyboards and style guides to decide on the visual look of the piece. This will help you be clear in your own mind what is going to be needed and possibly who you are going to need to collaborate with.

By the end of the planning stage you should have a clear set of documentation that describes in detail what you intend to produce. This will enable you to communicate your ideas to the client or to other members of your production team. If you are working alone and producing the work purely for yourself, you should still go through this stage to help you define your ideas clearly within your own mind.

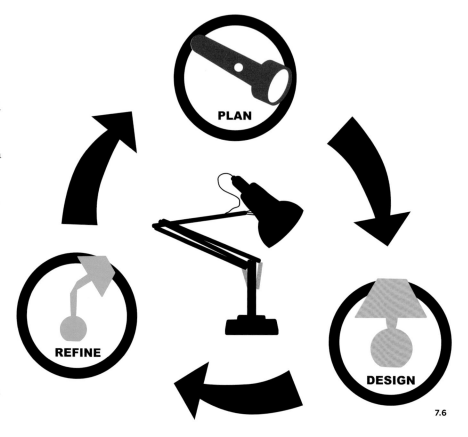

7.6 Plan, design, refine
The design process should follow a cyclical action. The stages are repeated, with each iteration getting closer to the finished result.

7.6

Designing

The design stage is where you begin actually producing material. Using the documents you created in the previous stage, work through the process of creating a first pass at the finished product. It does not matter at this point if it is not finished. The important point here is to get something made that can be viewed by others.

You may, through the process of actually creating, deviate from the ideas developed in the planning stage. Don't worry. This is fine, as long as what you are producing still fulfills the requirements of the original objective. This is a natural part of the creative process. You can continue to add variations to your initial idea and thus improve the finished piece.

At some point, however, you must stop. This will be the point when enough work has been completed for someone else to view and get a real sense of the finished project. It may be a little rough around the edges, but that is okay.

Refining

This is the point where you show your work to someone else. If you are producing it for a client, it would be good to show it to them at this point. If you are working as part of a team, take time to sit down and view the work together. If you are working alone, find someone else to look at it and give you his or her opinions. If none of these options are open, then leave the piece for a while (a day or so) and then come back to view it again yourself.

The purpose is to really think about what you have produced and what can be improved. Think about the technical aspects. Can the timings be tighter? Is the color as you want it? Do the visuals work with the sound? Does the visual composition work? Think also about the concept. Does it still communicate the message in the way that you intended? Look back at your original ideas and see if what you have produced still meets the objective.

Compile a list of things that need to be refined or improved. Order them with the things that are essential at the top and the things that are nonessential but would be nice at the bottom.

You now can begin the process again. Go back to the planning stage. Work out what needs to be done to implement the changes. Then move on to the designing stage to actually put the changes into practice. Finally, return to the refining stage to see if what you have produced needs any more work. Continue this cycle until you have no more refinements to make.

By sticking to this design process model you will ensure that the work that you produce has a solid underpinning. It may seem alien to do at first, but after a while it will simply become second nature.

THE PRODUCTION PIPELINE

When working on a motion graphic piece, whether you are working alone or as part of a larger organization, there is a sequence within which you must work to produce an effective end result. Some of this has been touched on in the section on the design process, where the order for designing was considered in its entirety from idea through to completion.

The order that the work is completed within the production phase is known as the *production pipeline*. It is made up of a series of discrete tasks, each one being completed in order, before moving on to the next. In a large organization it may well be that each stage on the pipeline is performed by a separate person or department. Often, in practice, one person will do more than one of the stages. Indeed, if you are working alone, you will be doing them all.

Regardless of how many people are involved in the pipeline, the process remains the same. It may help to think of it as a relay race with the project as the baton. Each stage must be run in its own right, but the important part is in the handover. The way in which the project is received and then subsequently handed on affects the smooth running of the project as a whole.

Pre-production

This is the work that is done before the project begins in order to ensure that everyone involved understands what is required. This will include concept design, storyboarding, and visual styling. This will be led by the **creative director**, whose role is to take overall control of the look and feel of the piece. They will liaise closely with the client (if there is one) to ensure that what is required is what is produced. There may well be a storyboard artist, someone who excels at sequential storytelling. It is important that the storyboard artist is aware of what is practical so that the ideas proposed are achievable. There may also be a **concept artist**, whose job it is to produce visuals that convey the idea prior to production.

It is important that all of the work produced in this stage is archived so that the rest of the team can refer to it. It is common practice to pin storyboards and concept art to the wall for constant reference.

Production

The work that is done during the production phase varies from project to project. Some of the stages of production will be similar across different projects. Other stages will be unique to a specific project.

The earliest stages may involve capture of video, so there will be a video production unit made up of multiple members, including a camera operator, lighting and sound director, and so forth. It is important for someone like the creative director to be on the shoot also in order to take reference photographs and to observe what is shot. This person can then make suggestions that may make the subsequent stages simpler. If there are likely to be any visual effects, a **visual effects coordinator** should be on set. It is this person's job to ensure that all of the subsequent stages work well together. There may also be a photographer on set to ensure that the context of the shoot is well documented. Their photographs will be used as reference material later on. For example, images of the surrounding landscape or the lighting on set can be used to help recreate consistent virtual environments.

There may not be a need for any underlying video footage, in which case the visual designer would begin making reference to the material generated earlier. Individual assets need to be created, whether they are physical, photographic, or digital. The exact form that these should take needs to be agreed on beforehand. It is no good creating a highly detailed model if it is only going to appear in the shot at a distance or for a short period of time. Similarly, it would be a disaster to create visual elements at the wrong size or resolution for the intended final use. Communication and documentation are essential.

If the project is to include any CGI elements, it is at this point that the modeler, rigger, texture artist, lighter, and animator would produce their work. They would work under the supervision of the creative director and/or the visual effects coordinator to ensure that the assets are developed as required.

Post-production

At this point all of the assets have been created. A **data wrangler** will ensure that all of the individual elements are saved, labeled, and organized so that others can easily access them. They should also ensure that all are backed up and stored in a separate location. There is nothing worse than having to recreate lost elements.

Now the **editor** cuts together any underlying video footage. Once this is completed satisfactorily the **compositor** blends all the elements together. This may simply consist of ensuring that elements are pasted on top of each other, utilizing masking or blending modes to ensure that they give the impression of being part of the same image. It may involve multiple masks and a variety of keying techniques to achieve the desired result. It may also require animation techniques, separate from those in the production phase.

Ideally, once the piece is completed in its initial state, it should be checked by the director and the client. Any changes are sent back down to the relevant part of the pipeline and once complete, sent back up through each stage. The process is repeated until the work is complete, at which point it would be rendered out in the desired final format.

7.7

7.7 The 4Ds method

The design agency The Neighbourhood from Manchester, UK, employs the 4Ds method in their production pipeline. These are Discover (find out what the client wants and what the scope of the brief is), Define (begin to work out creative solutions to the problem), Design (iteratively produce work that moves toward a final solution), Deliver (produce any finishing touches and hand over to the client while assessing the success of the project in order to learn from it for future projects).

www.the-neighbourhood.com

CHAPTER EIGHT
PROCESS:
PRODUCTION

We have covered in detail elsewhere in this book the actual techniques used within a production. We have seen that they are many and varied, and a motion graphics project may consist of a variety of production processes depending on what the desired end result may be.

Within this chapter, we will look at the production process in more general terms and discuss many of the aspects, methods, and techniques that you can employ regardless of production method.

We will discuss the things you should consider when working with video, whether you are shooting it yourself or acquiring it from another source. We will also consider the issue of copyright and what you can do to ensure you don't fall afoul of the law and how to protect your work. We will look at the important topic of media management and discuss the importance of understanding different output codecs and standards for your moving images, as well as the technique of prototyping and how you can use it with motion graphics. Finally, we will discuss things you should consider when working in teams.

8.1 Path

The features of the Path social messaging platform are illustrated in this promotional film by Paul Trillo. Actors perform in front of a screen onto which animated backgrounds are projected live. New visual elements appear on cue, as the display is engineered to be controlled by the filmmakers using game engine software.

Visual design, video production, animation, performance, stage management, and programming had to be coordinated in order to produce the elegant and deceptively simple film.

http://paultrillo.com

SHOOTING VIDEO

Video material will be vital to many of the motion graphics sequences you produce. The video material may be supplied by somebody else, shot by an individual or agency in accordance with carefully specified requirements, such as file format, resolution, composition, screen-direction, and so forth. Alternatively, you may receive or request stock or library footage that was shot some time previously. You may also be called upon to shoot some video yourself.

Video production is a complex process; before undertaking a video shoot, it is worth considering several of these complexities.

Video is assembly

Video sequences are not simply the ad hoc recording of a live, continuous performance; video sequences are constructed, like a jigsaw, from individually staged and composed shots. Often the same on-screen events are reenacted and re-recorded from a variety of positions, so that a number of alternative perspectives on events are available in the editing stage. Editing involves the review, organization, and assembly of the most appropriate shots.

It is unwise to regard editing as "salvage" work, picking over the debris of a recording in search of "treasure." Instead, the editing stage should be viewed as systematically sewing together the different panels of a tailored shirt; the arrangement and sequence of the shots will have been predetermined with care.

When assembled, the shots accumulate to create a coherent flow of visual information. Each portion of key visual information must be clearly depicted before it is rapidly replaced with new visual information.

Visual grammar

Just like spoken or written language, video and film are governed by a set of rules and principles that guide how individual shots should be composed and how they should be arranged in a sequence. This "visual grammar" (also known as *film language*) requires that each progressive clip in a video sequence is produced with an awareness of how the current visual information must be replaced by new, relevant visual information. When visual grammar is evident, the viewer experiences a flow of seemingly continuous and interrelated shots. The viewer becomes almost oblivious to the shots' disjointed nature. Without visual grammar, the video may seem discontinuous and artificial, and its assembly may be jarringly conspicuous.

SHOOTING
VIDEO

MEDIA
MANAGEMENT   PROTOTYPING   WORKING
WITH OTHERS   COPYRIGHT

CASE STUDY:
TENDRIL

Shot distance

One important principle of visual grammar is the concept of *shot distance*. Shot distance describes the extent to which the subject of a shot (typically a human) fills the frame. For example, if the film story requires that the viewer can immediately recognize the setting of events, the sequence would begin with a *wide shot* (WS) to establish the environment that surrounds the character. If we must reveal the precise identity of the character, the shot would be framed so that his or her face almost fills the frame; this shot distance is called a *close up* (CU). If the character is revealed to be engaged in some kind of activity, such as soldering or golf, then an upper-body shot (*mid-shot*, MS), or full-body shot (*full shot*, FS) would be presented. What we leave out of the frame is as important as what we leave in. Appropriate shot distances give emphasis to the relevant piece of new visual information.

Technical competence

Modern cameras and camcorders are very sophisticated and intelligent devices. They are capable of making fully autonomous decisions about exposure, focus, and **white balance**. They can automatically attenuate the level at which audio is recorded in response to changes in sound level. However, thus far, no camera is fully capable of mind-reading; no camcorder can accurately estimate your intentions. We will still have to make most of the decisions about camera position and composition since these two crucial aspects of a shot do not have a convenient automatic setting.

In addition, we will have to accept or reject all of the technical decisions regarding focus, exposure, and color because the camcorder will usually make decisions based on average values or centrally positioned elements.

Other aspects of a video shoot require the same degree of critical validation. Microphone placement, environmental acoustics, and interference cannot be accurately identified and acted upon by the press of a button.

The limits of the camera

Furthermore, cameras are not as adept as the human eye at determining the full spectrum of visible tones. Their tone perception is far narrower than we perceive, so it is inevitable that some kind of lighting design will be called for. This may be as simple as using a reflector or *bounce-board* to redirect some of the available light back toward the under-illuminated regions of the subject.

Much more elaborate lighting setups may be required, especially if a chroma-key background is a factor.

Recording acceptable footage requires a degree of technical and aesthetic understanding and competence that should not be underestimated. For this reason, many motion design agencies have formed professional partnerships with experts in video production.

MEDIA MANAGEMENT

Consider all the potential ingredients of a motion graphic: multiple video elements may be composited, animations may be derived from sequences of still images, music and speech may be added, additional sound effects may combine to create the illusion that artificial elements are realistic, custom font files may be required, batch script files may be utilized to automate certain animations, external plugin filters or effects may be exploited. The list is expansive. It is no exaggeration to state that a single motion graphic movie, even one as short as a few seconds, may be comprised of dozens, hundreds, or even thousands of different media components.

Offline media

Now consider this potential nightmare scenario: You launch a multimedia project in your preferred application, only to be presented with a warning that one or more of these manifold items is **offline**. This means that these items that the project depends on have been deleted or moved from their original location on the computer.

Recovering the lost media can be frustrating, time consuming, and very disruptive to the production workflow. This is why professional practitioners take great care to plan and respect an agreed and consistent method of storing, naming, and locating all of the dependant media. This discipline is called *media management* or *digital asset management* (**DAM**).

Media management is an important aspect of the production workflow. A media management method must be sensitive to and consistent with the agreed methods of the following:

- specifying media formats for each stage of production

- acquiring media

- naming media

- attaching relevant metadata

- storing the media in a sensible location

- backing up files in an additional location

- exporting and publishing draft and final products in agreed formats to agreed locations

- delivering media in the stipulated formats

SHOOTING
VIDEO

MEDIA
MANAGEMENT

PROTOTYPING

WORKING
WITH OTHERS

COPYRIGHT

CASE STUDY:
TENDRIL

Media management in teams

Most animation, video-compositing, and editing software applications will impose their own preferred structures for storing and managing project media. Some software can consolidate all utilized media into a single directory and jettison any redundant media that is no longer in use. As a sole user of a single computer, perhaps your own laptop or workstation, you may be fortunate to have a single, local directory into which all of your documents are deposited with no real intervention on your part.

It is rare for a single user to experience disconnection between a project and the assets utilized within it. However, in the media industry, the storage of an important project on a sole, vulnerable device would be very risky. Typically, media assets are stored on high specification media-server computers so that they can be accessed by more than one person on different workstations in the post-production facility.

On some jobs, different members of the creative team may be working on parallel projects that reference the same underlying media. This is why a uniform protocol for managing the underlying media should be designed for and enforced by all stakeholders. It is also common practice never to willfully delete a media asset unless two backups of the file are known to reside elsewhere.

Media management is not something that happens in the midst of or at the end of a project. It should be a tactical and disciplined feature of your professional approach to media production.

PROTOTYPING

Prototyping is the process by which early, unpolished versions of a finished product are produced to enable the developer to see how things are working and to better communicate their vision to a client. It is a means of giving an idea of what the finished piece will look like without actually going to all the hard work of making it.

Within motion graphics the work is often created in a highly polished state from the outset. There are processes, however, that can be employed to ease the communication of those ideas prior to beginning final production.

Paper prototyping

All design work should begin on paper.

It is important to understand and communicate what the motion will be. Because it is difficult to do this using words alone, the storyboard is an essential tool. A storyboard is a sequential set of images that shows the progression of the motion. It should give an indication of the framing of each shot as well as describe how the elements will move within the frame. It should also show any camera moves. It is not necessary that it is beautifully drawn or colored correctly. Its purpose is purely to communicate how things move. Simple shapes with directional arrows will do.

Often, when deciding how a motion will progress, changes are made to the sequence. With this in mind it is a good idea to create each "frame" on a separate piece of paper. This is often done on small postcard-sized cards or even on sticky notes. This way, the motion sequence can easily be reorganized or entirely new sequences inserted. For team projects, the storyboard is often placed on the wall for easy reference.

As well as storyboards, you might produce colored mockups of the final look. These can be done on a computer in the software you will be using, but could just as easily be done using traditional art materials. The purpose here is not to show exactly what the finished piece will be like but to give an impression of what the "feel" will be. You will be able to try out a variety of colorings and tonality before you commit to the final version.

TIP | A MOVING PROTOTYPE

Motion graphics is often employed by software developers to prototype their applications. Through the use of animation a client or user can be shown a simulation of the application working that helps to explain the process much more clearly than words alone. The animation can be produced using animation software that does not allow for interaction, but is a much quicker way of producing motion.

SHOOTING
VIDEO

MEDIA
MANAGEMENT

PROTOTYPING

WORKING
WITH OTHERS

COPYRIGHT

CASE STUDY:
TENDRIL

Visual prototyping

This stage would come after a paper prototype. This is the point when you would begin to create things on-screen to better explain how the finished product will look. A good first step is to produce an **animatic**. This begins with a drawn storyboard. Each frame is then digitized into the computer and placed on a timeline. The duration of each frame is altered to correspond with the intended duration of the finished sequence. If there are any camera movements, these can be recreated on screen. This takes the static storyboard, with its emphasis on direction of movement, and adds the dimension of time. It is effectively an animated storyboard.

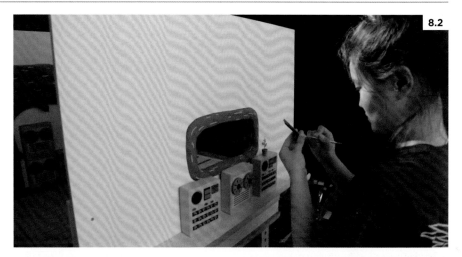

8.2 Communicating ideas
The production process for this Nexus Productions commercial for Dorset Cereals began with a storyboard, which everyone working on the project could refer to. This enabled the ideas of the director to be communicated to the artists (top and middle) ensuring that the finished product (bottom) is as close to the original vision as possible.

www.nexusproductions.com

WORKING WITH OTHERS

Although team-working skills are prized by employers, we must not assume that teamwork is always the best approach to a task. Psychologists have identified that in some situations individuals will work less hard toward a goal if they are part of a team; this phenomenon is known as *social loafing*. Teams can also take longer to solve problems, although their solutions are usually better than individual ones. Yet, there are times when collaboration is the most appropriate working method.

By working in a team, we can be more efficient, produce better solutions to problems, and capitalize on a range of diverse skills and expertise. Much of the actual work may still be conducted in parallel isolation, but teams will need to come together for discussion, decision making, problem solving, and planning.

In the creative industries, teams with a fusion of adaptable technical skills, communication skills, and entrepreneurial skills are believed to be the most resilient to the rapidly changing landscape of media and commerce. Few individuals possess all of these attributes, so membership on a team also offers us some security. Teamwork can also be positive for morale and job satisfaction.

8.3

SHOOTING
VIDEO

MEDIA
MANAGEMENT   PROTOTYPING

WORKING
WITH OTHERS

COPYRIGHT

CASE STUDY:
TENDRIL

Effective teams

Simply labeling a group of people in a department or shared workspace a team does not *make* them a team. To become an effective team, the group must subscribe to a shared goal. A team leader is necessary to shape our approach to the task, with input on this from team members who will then work together toward this collective goal.

In addition to our goal-relevant credentials, we must also be as committed to team well-being as we are to task completion and quality. If we are all truly invested in producing the best possible work, and we recognize that a collaborative effort is required for this, then there is no room for ego or selfish, private objectives. All team members must be concerned with the challenges faced by all other members, and with overcoming these for the benefit of the team.

Conflict in teams

There must be no confusion or ambiguity about what the common objective is. A lack of consensus about the purpose of the team will be a significant cause of conflict. Conflict is also likely to arise if there are disagreements about how this goal should be approached; for example, if individuals feel that the allocation of work is not equitable. Another major source of conflict in teams is personal conflict.

Personality clashes in a team are as inevitable as clashes in any relationship. When conflict arises, there are several ways of dealing with it. Denial or avoiding the conflict will serve only to postpone an inevitable clash. A head-on battle with the counterpart will make others uncomfortable, and compromises on either side can lead to resentment. Effective teams are emotionally mature and able to resolve conflict quickly and professionally, so the recommended approach to resolve interpersonal tensions in a team is to articulate your negative feelings without overtly expressing them. It can be difficult to separate the conflict from the parties involved, but this may be necessary to come up with an objective solution that appeals to everyone. For more advice on how to tackle conflict in teams, please see www.bloomsbury.com/crook-motion-graphics.

8.3 Teamwork
Being an effective part of a team is a necessary and enjoyable part of any creative discipline.

COPYRIGHT

Creative individuals and organizations expend a great deal of imagination, time, and energy in order to produce creative works such as music, animation, theater, architecture, dance, paintings, photography, and film. These works—each one an item of *intellectual property*—may be more valuable than any material property. Like material possessions, intellectual property can be sold or leased. It can also be stolen. Fortunately, copyright laws offer a legal framework for the protection and control of intellectual property. In the production of a motion graphic, we may exploit a number of copyrighted components, but we must not infringe the rights of the copyright holders.

The copyright of a work (i.e., the right to control if and how it may be copied) is initially owned by its creator. However, copyright is often transferred to another body, such as an employer or publisher, and this body can prohibit or selectively permit the reproduction of the material.

8.4

8.4 The Free Music Archive
Locating media online is not difficult. However, the ability to download media does not grant us the right to reproduce or commercially exploit the material.

The Free Music Archive is a curated library of legal music downloads. Many of the music tracks are accompanied by a Creative Commons license: an unambiguously expressed contract that clearly states how the music may be used.

http://freemusicarchive.org

SHOOTING
VIDEO

MEDIA
MANAGEMENT   PROTOTYPING

WORKING
WITH OTHERS

COPYRIGHT

CASE STUDY:
TENDRIL

Digital type

One kind of computer program that motion graphic designers will frequently use is font software, necessary to render digital type. A font file is actually a small computer program that describes how the outline of each of the letterforms may be "drawn" by multimedia or word-processing applications. Because the software is the result of the skillful arrangement of words (albeit computer code), a font is subject to the same copyright protection as literary works such as poems, novels, and song lyrics. When the font is installed onto the computer (which may occur at the same time as the operating system installation), the user is required to agree to a license. This license dictates how many computers the font software may be installed upon, and may also restrict the number of locations of these computers.

As long as a letterform is selectable and editable, the computer is referring to the underlying code that describes how to display it. Once the text is exported as a movie file, the information about those letterforms is reduced to the mere appearance of pixels on a screen; thus, the underlying font file is no longer in use. However, in some countries, the actual appearance of a typeface is also protected by copyright as an artistic work, irrespective of whether the type is generated by the font file or by any other means, such as tracing or photography.

Our obligations

The World Wide Web abounds with music, video, and digital imagery, as well as software and fonts. Although these may be easily located and downloaded, we must never surmise that this availability equates to permission to use them in any way we decide. Each of these items is the intellectual property of another, and we must respect their right to decide how and where the item may be used, and if it may be adapted.

There are no moral or legal exceptions to the rights of creators. A student of motion graphics (or any other discipline) is not exempt from the moral and legal aspects of copyright. There are some exceptions that permit limited duplication of items for private study, but this does not extend to the unrestricted use of copyrighted works in an educational setting. If we expect our own work to be treated with respect, we must—even as students—acknowledge the ownership of a creative work and never use it without permission.

CASE STUDY:
TENDRIL

Tendril is an animation and design studio based in Toronto, Canada.

Tendril's studio is a lab and workshop where directors, designers, and artists from diverse backgrounds come together to create "powerful visual storytelling experiences."

They employ a wide range of styles and techniques, and have produced work for the likes of Pepsi, Nike, Samsung, and Toyota.

We asked the team at Tendril about what they do and how they do it together.

How fully does the term "motion graphics" describe what Tendril does?
The definition of the term motion graphics seems to always be expanding. Or maybe it's just that the people doing motion graphics have kept evolving, trying out new things, and expanding their craft and interests into new areas. I guess we wouldn't limit ourselves to just that term. At our studio, beyond motion graphics, design, and animation, we also focus on interactive experiences, games, live action, and solid storytelling—which all sometimes involve motion graphics, but not always.

8.5–8.6 Tendril
The team at Tendril is a collective of experts in CGI, animation, filmmaking, and interactivity. They often collaborate with creative partners in different countries and time zones to produce work for international clients.

8.5

THE
CAMERA

MEDIA
MANAGEMENT   PROTOTYPING

WORKING
WITH OTHERS   COPYRIGHT

CASE STUDY:
TENDRIL

Is everything done in-house or do you ever have to work with external partners?

We collaborate in some capacity on each and every project we create. Even when something is done entirely with in-studio staff and resources, we are collaborating with a client and/or agency.

Collaboration is really at the very core of what we do. We often join forces with gaming companies, interactive companies, talented directors, and other amazing studios that are not a direct part of Tendril. Working with external partners is never a shortcoming though—it only makes a project richer.

We also have two sister companies we share a space with—Relish Editing and 567 Visual Effects—and we sometimes collaborate with them to take our projects to the next level of polish.

Are the individuals who work at Tendril multiskilled generalists or experts in a single discipline?

Each person at Tendril tends to have a speciality or thing they do incredibly well while also being a well-rounded and competent generalist. The reality is that there's not always a project going on that suits someone's very strongest skill set, so we all have to be good at many stages of the process to help each other out. When something arises that really speaks to a person's main expertise, we make sure they're totally on deck to let their talents really shine.

What are the most important craft skills that entrants to this field should possess?

Really, we all agree that so long as you're savvy, anything can be self-taught via Google or YouTube tutorials.

In fact, almost all of us at Tendril are largely self-taught [with] totally diverse backgrounds like biology, engineering, philosophy, literature, and architecture. The learning continues for all of us daily as we share new ideas and techniques and learn from mistakes we make along the way. In some ways a healthy studio environment is like a school.

On the pure craft side of things, mastering the software tools of the trade—at least one 2D design and animation software tool and one 3D tool—ensures that your basic skills don't frustrate your creative motivations.

8.6

8.7

THE
CAMERA

MEDIA
MANAGEMENT PROTOTYPING

WORKING
WITH OTHERS COPYRIGHT

CASE STUDY:
TENDRIL

What are the most important "soft" or transferable skills that entrants to this field should possess?

True passion and hunger to create better work and generally be [a] great person to those around you are the most critical general attributes anyone in this field should have.

That hunger needs to be backed up by *focus* and an incredible work ethic. Also: teamwork, problem solving, staying cool under pressure, and time management all the way.

What are the pleasures of working together on a project?

Animation, gaming, and filmmaking all thrive on cross-pollination and team efforts. We are the sum of our parts. We function as a team, and we really couldn't do it any other way.

Plus, all the jokes and the ping-pong playing to decompress help carry us past any stressful days. Put simply, it's way more fun than working in a bubble of solitude.

What are the challenges of working across a multidisciplinary project, and how do you deal with these?

Just being literate enough to be competent across multiple disciplines is a huge challenge. It's really important in these cases to understand where the skills are (and who has them on the team) so that everyone is doing the thing that is best suited for the task at hand. That said, it's also important to us to let everyone try new things and to be understanding and compassionate if they aren't perfect the first time round. Study, study, study—and ask lots of questions.

Clearly planning out complicated projects from the get-go and having technical meetings to weed out potential pitfalls before falling into them is great too.

What are the most important tools for ensuring an efficient workflow?

In a word: producers!

We are always looking for ways to improve workflow. A well-organized and understood file structure for projects is essential. This file structure is usually built on the working process and stages of a particular discipline (i.e., a 2D animation versus 3D animation approach).

Beyond that, effective communication, task tracking, and project management are facilitated with software tools like Google Docs, Slack, and Trello.

Artists are liberated when they have clear goals, lists, and priorities. The challenge with some apps (like Slack or Skype, or even email) is to know when to tune out and focus, as there is a constant stream of noise that may or may not be relevant to the work you need to accomplish.

www.tendril.ca

8.7 A creative environment
Inspiration and works in progress adorn the walls of the Toronto-based studio.

CONCLUSION

This book explores a broad range of technological principles and software tools, but it also considers the competences and personal attributes of a designer. We began by finding out how moving images are constructed, composed, and manipulated. We learned how to articulate complex notions, such as the movement of objects in space and time. We then explored how to bring together various media in different ways in order to create motion graphics, before looking back over the process to consider all of the different stages and tasks as part of a coherent and organized process. Along the way, professionals have given us their perspective on what is important in the practice of motion graphics.

Motion graphics is a synthesis of a variety of disciplines. At different times, a motion graphic designer may perform any number of various roles: artist, graphic designer, typographer, animator, filmmaker, storyteller, instructor, and project manager. Motion graphics demands versatility and flexibility.

We hope that you have found this book to be interesting and useful, and that you are inspired to continue investigating the numerous aspects of motion graphic design. In the following sections, we recommend a few books and websites for you to consider reading or visiting. We hope that some of the more complicated aspects of motion graphic design will now be a little more understandable and accessible to you.

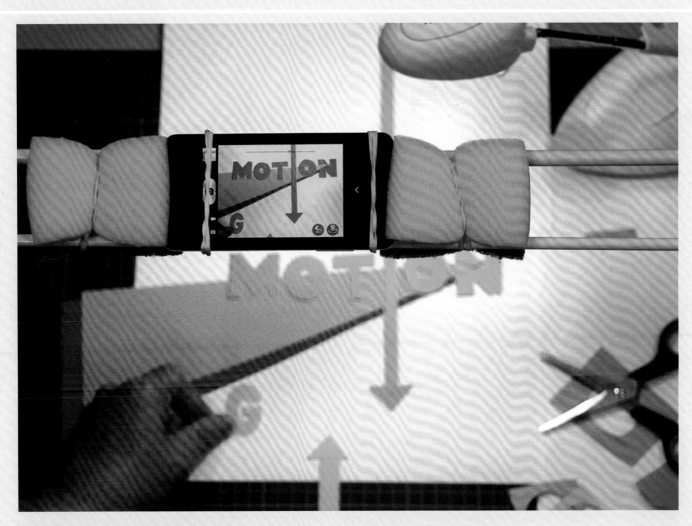

Getting started with motion graphics

We hope you have discovered that creating
motion graphics does not depend on the latest
fancy software and hardware. With very modest
tools, such as smartphones and craft materials,
it is possible to begin to experiment with shape,
color, type, and motion. So get started!

Please see www.bloomsbury.com/crook-motion-
graphics for more on this project.

GLOSSARY

2.5D
Two-and-a-half-D. This is a method of creating the illusion of a three-dimensional moving image from a two-dimensional image. Typically, a photograph is selectively expanded into receding image planes. Differentiated motion is applied to each plane, creating a *parallax* effect.

ADR
Automated Dialogue Replacement. A method of replacing substandard dialogue in video material. Actors in a sound booth review their performance, which may initially have been captured in a noisy or reverberant setting, in order to recreate their vocal performance.

After Effects
Video editing and compositing software from Adobe Systems that is used extensively in motion graphic production.

AI
AI can refer to the vector-image application Adobe Illustrator, or to the file format and file-name extension of the object-oriented files it is used to create. AI files are widely supported by compositing applications and text-generators.

Alpha Channel
Whereas the color information in an image or video is stored in red, green, and blue color channels, the alpha channel stores information about the transparent, or "invisible," parts of the visual data.

Animatic
Somewhat like an animated storyboard. A low-fidelity "mockup" of a narrative animation or video sequence. An animatic may be used at the pitching and commissioning stage of a project, or in the iterative production of a final, polished product.

Armature
In traditional stop-motion animation, an armature is the mechanical skeleton of a figure. This can be subtly adjusted, moment by moment, in order to create the incremental postures of an animated movement.

Aspect Ratio
A proportional relationship between the width and height of a canvas, screen, or image, usually expressed as a ratio (e.g, 16:9).

Cell
In traditional animation, a cell is a transparent sheet onto which one frame of an animated character is painted. The sheet is then placed over a static background image. In computer animation, this is analogous to a layer on a timeline.

Chroma
The color component of an image or video. *Chroma-keying* exploits a nominated range (or hue) of the chroma information in order to remove or replace (*key*) part of the visual information.

Codec
Meaning "compressor-decompressor," a codec is a set of standards that describes how digital hardware and software can reduce the size of media data and subsequently reconstitute it.

Color Grading
A stage of film/video post-production in which video footage is manipulated so that colors are conformed, subdued, subverted, or emphasized.

Compositing
The process of layering and blending multiple video and image media into a single video clip.

Compositor
The person employed to undertake the compositing on a project, or the software used to do that process.

Concept Artist
A creative person brought in at the beginning of a project to communicate visual ideas of how a finished piece may look.

Connotation
In communication studies, connotation describes the implied meaning or associations of an image, word, or other symbol. Often contrasted with *denotation*, which corresponds to that which is literally depicted.

Copyright Clearance
When you have acquired formal permission to reproduce music, images, video, film, writing, or other copyrighted works, you have obtained clearance.

Creative Commons
A licensing system that allows creators to make clear how their work may be reproduced without clearance being obtained.

Creative Director
The person who has overall control over the look and feel of a finished piece. They will usually negotiate between the client and the production team.

DAM
Digital Asset Management. The specification and workflow of how multiple, disparate media files should be organized and handled during a project.

Data Wrangler
The person responsible for ensuring that digital media is correctly duplicated, organized, named, and labeled.

Denotation
See *Connotation*.

Depth of Field
The range in which objects at a diminishing proximity to the camera lens will appear to be in focus. The deeper the depth of field, the greater the territory over which close and distant objects are all in focus.

Dope Sheet
A planning document used in animation in which all the required movement of character components is plotted in a frame-by-frame chart. Dope sheets are particularly important for deconstructing synchronized dialogue into moment-by-moment mouth positions.

Editor
The person who cuts a film sequence together. They may not be the same person who performs the compositing or other visual effects.

EPS
Encapsulated PostScript. A file format in which a vector image is often stored.

Foley
A method of fabricating in post-production the nonspeech sounds that accompany moving images. The noise of household implements and specially designed contraptions are synchronized credibly with footsteps, punches, explosions, and other apparent sources of sound on the screen.

Font
A digital file that contains information about how a letterform in a particular typeface (or *font family*) should be rendered by computer software.

Frame
Either the boundary of the image plane (a single image in a moving image sequence) or the location in time of that individual image.

Frame-rate
The rate at which individual frames appear on screen. Commonly, video works at a frame-rate of 25 frames per second (fps), hence 1 second of video will contain 25 separate frames. It is possible to customize a frame-rate to suit your needs, e.g., a web animation could display at 1 fps.

Gamma
Gamma describes the mid-value of a spectrum of tones in an image or video display. Gamma adjustment is sometimes required for the tones to appear correctly distributed across the spectrum. Gamma adjustment has the effect of altering or correcting mid-tones without affecting bright or dark values.

GIF
Graphics Interchange Format. A raster image file format used widely on the World Wide Web as it will store information about a sequence of images; hence, it is capable of rendering simple animations. However, GIFs cannot resolve as much color information as a JPEG or PNG image.

GIMP
GNU Image Manipulation Program. A free, open-source alternative to Adobe Photoshop.

H.264
An effective video compression format that is utilized by Blu-ray video systems, as well as streaming services such as YouTube, Vimeo, and iTunes. Many professional camcorders also shoot in this format.

Image Plane
When three-dimensional objects are rendered, projected, or perceived on a two-dimensional screen or canvas, the point at which this occurs, and the corresponding depiction of flattened objects upon it, is known as the image plane.

Interpolation

Interpolation is a mathematical process whereby one compound or intermediate number is derived from two other numbers. Interpolation may be used by multimedia software to calculate the color or position of an as yet nonexistent element (such as a pixel or coordinate of a vector) by comparing or combining two supplied values.

Iteration

To iterate is to repeat, to refine, and to revisit. Iteration is good practice in the execution of any creative endeavor and is often used to describe the design process.

JPEG

The Joint Photographic Experts Group. A committee of specialists who develop international standards for compression image data, most frequently utilized in the image file format named after them.

Key-frame

A frame in a sequence that describes a critical position, size, or shape of an animated object. The full sequence is generated with reference to nearby key-frames; intermediate frames are estimated based on their differences.

Keying

The process of replacing certain spatial regions of a moving image with substitute footage. Chroma-keying is a familiar method, whereby the green background areas of the video are replaced with the image of an alternative setting.

Kinetic

Energy exhibited by a moving object.

Kinetic Type

A genre of motion graphics in which type animates acrobatically as the corresponding words are sung or spoken.

Light Box

An illuminated desk on which animators will trace underlying drawings to create the next drawing in a sequence.

Metadata

All digitally generated files are embedded with small pieces of textual or numerical information that describe various parameters such as duration and creation date. This "data about the data" is called metadata, and can be edited or supplemented with any useful information regarding the media content, quality, or origin.

Motion Blur

An optical side effect of photographic and video technology, which means that fast-moving objects cannot be sharply delineated in each frame of video. Although this limitation does not apply when creating CGI objects, motion blur is sometimes added to emulate what has become a familiar visual artifact of moving images.

Motionographer

A person undertaking the act of creating motion graphics.

Motion Path

A reference path created in animation software to indicate the trajectory over which a moving object will traverse.

MPEG

The Motion Picture Expert Group. A body that researches and defines international standards for multimedia file formats. It gave its name to several widely used movie file formats.

Node-based

An alternative interface to timeline-based tools. In node-based authoring software, a logical flowchart of animated events, behaviors, and interactions is created and enacted.

Nuke

Widely used compositing software. Nuke is node-based, unlike timeline-based software such as After Effects or Flash.

Offline

When a digital media file is in a different location than where the software expects to find it. Media may be strategically left offline, so that components are reunited at a later stage in the production. Frequently, media is offline by mistake because of poor media management.

Onion Skinning

A feature in animation software that inspects the differing positions and shapes of an animated object across a sequence of frames and then displays these all in a single frame.

Open Source

Software that allows users to inspect and adapt code without restriction.

Parallax

The appearance of nearby objects moving across the image plane faster than distant objects.

Particle Systems

Some types of complex and random visual phenomena such as smoke, waves, and flames would be tremendously complex to animate using conventional frame-by-frame or tweened animation. Particle systems enable such occurrences to be simulated in CGI and compositing software. Physical parameters, such as origin, velocity, direction, and mass are specified; these are used to create and propagate the molecular coordinates of a fluid and dynamic mass.

Persistence of Vision

Because of this psychological phenomenon, one of a series of rapidly presented still images will reside in the visual memory until it is replaced. It is for this reason that we experience film and video as a continuous experience, rather than a jarring bombardment of distinct images.

Piece-to-Camera

A video consisting of a single performer talking directly to the camera.

Pixel

A single color component among thousands or millions of neighboring color "tiles" that together create the illusion of a continuous-tone image, photograph, or frame of video.

PNG

Portable Network Graphic. A still-image file format that is used widely in multimedia production, as it can discern full RGB color information while using a compression method that does not degrade the image quality as much as the JPEG format.

Point Cloud

A group of coordinates used by CGI software to delineate the form or surface of a complex three-dimensional object. Stick several dozen dressmaking pins into the surface of a tangerine—the mass of pinheads is equivalent to a point cloud.

Pre-Viz

Pre-Visualization. Another term to describe a low-fidelity "blueprint" of a moving image sequence, such as an animatic, used for reference during the final production stages.

Proprietary

Software for which the use, adaptation, and duplication is restricted.

Protagonist

The main character or hero in a story; the person with a goal to accomplish or problem to overcome.

PSD

The file-name extension by which images created in Adobe Photoshop may be identified. The format is widely supported by media-production software; this support is not isolated to Adobe products.

Raster Image

An image comprised of rows and columns of pixels.

Render

In the following situations and others, we are creating media that had not previously existed: when we composite two or more video clips; when we superimpose text over video; when we use modeling software to prescribe the position and movement of objects, virtual cameras, and light sources; and when we establish a tween by defining the outermost key-frames of an animation. Computer software uses our instructions and source media to generate the new media. This is called *rendering*.

Resolution

The number of picture elements that occupy a common unit of display territory; usually measured in *pixels per inch* for screen-based media and *dots per inch* for print-based media. When images are used across media of varying dimensions, resolution is the attribute that ensures sufficient fine detail is *resolved* in the image.

RGB

Red, Green, and Blue. The additive primary colors that form the minuscule color-emitting elements of a video screen, as well as the color constituents of each pixel in a digital image intended for display on such devices.

RGBA

An extended RGB image file format that, as well as including information about the visible colors' components, also includes data regarding transparency (or *alpha*).

Rig

A computer-generated skeleton that replicates a traditional animation armature. It is the scaffold around which CGI characters are built and manipulated.

Rotoscoping

A technique in which a live-action recording of a moving object is traced over frame by frame to create an analogous animation.

Royalty
When copyrighted material is licensed, the copyright holder may demand a small payment for each instance of reproduction (e.g., for each broadcast of a commercial, for each sale of a DVD). If a flat fee is charged for unlimited reproduction, the material is *royalty-free*.

Sprite
In computer terms, a sprite is a self-contained, reusable design element. It can be any size or shape and may be a static image or an animated clip. The sprite is often manipulated by software to move around the screen and possibly to interact with other elements.

Stop-motion
A method of animation in which the illusion of continuous movement is created. A model or object is, frame by frame, moved fractionally and photographed to create the multiple images of the moving image sequence.

Storyboards
A paper-based plan of the appearance of a video-based sequence. By illustrating the significant events in a moving image, storyboards communicate how the final video sequence should be composed as well as how moving elements will enter, exit, and move within the frame.

TARGA
A legacy file format for digital images, one of the first file formats supported by video-editing software. TARGA supports alpha transparency, so it is a useful, portable, cross-platform format.

Timeline
Part of a time-based media player or editing application. A linear visual analogy for the series of adjacent frames that host the separate objects or images in the moving image.

Tracking
Unlike *motion-tracking*, tracking is an attribute of digital type. It describes how "spread out" a line of text appears, or how much space exists between each character.

Tweening
A tween describes the progressive estimation and generation of the position, size, or shape of an animated object across a number of frames between key-frames.

Vector Image
A type of image file format that uses geometry to describe the shape, color, and position of multiple objects. EPS and AI are common types of vector file formats.

Visual Effects Coordinator
The person responsible for overseeing the production of the VFX. This person will liaise between the video production team and the post-production teams.

VFX
Visual Effects. A branch of media production concerned with enhancing or manipulating film or video footage.

White Balance
The process by which a camera estimates, or is instructed, about the prevailing color of the light present. Otherwise, video cameras are naïve about the subtly different hues of light (from daylight to fluorescent strip lighting) in which video may be recorded.

YUV
Whereas digital images are created in RGB format, many video formats reconstitute these color components to calculate luminance (brightness) information (Y) and two-color comparison signals (U, V). The YUV signal is more succinct, but can be used to rebuild the RGB data.

FURTHER READING
Books

Betancourt, M. (2013), *The History of Motion Graphics*, Rockville, Md.: Wildside Press.
A thorough grounding in the cultural history of motion graphics. The emphasis is on experimental abstract works, such as the innovative works of early avant-garde photographers and animators prior to the emergence of computer-based editing systems.

Braha, Y. and B. Byrne, (2010), *Creative Motion Graphic Titling for Film, Video, and the Web: Dynamic Motion Graphic Title Design* (Pap/Dvdr.), Waltham, Mass.: Focal Press.
A comprehensive overview of motion graphics concepts and processes, which is structured around the production workflow. It is a very appropriate next step following the book you are currently reading.

Brereton, R. (2009), *Sketchbooks: The Hidden Art of Designers, Illustrators & Creatives*, London: Laurence King.
A collection of revealing and inspirational interviews with artists and designers from different fields in which they show and explain how sketching is a part of their process.

Curran, S. (2001), *Motion Graphics: Graphic Design for Broadcast and Film*, Minneapolis: Rockport Publishers, Inc.
This thoughtful book considers the communicative intentions behind many recognizable case studies.

Kane, J. (2002), *A Type Primer*, London: Laurence King.
A thorough explanation of how typography has evolved into a design system that we use today. You will feel like a typography scholar after reading this book.

Krasner, J. S. (2008), *Motion Graphic Design: Applied History and Aesthetics*, 2nd edn, London: Focal.
A visually rich compendium of motion graphic work. It has some challenging exercises to consolidate the topics of each chapter. You will benefit most from this book if you are willing to read it from cover to cover, rather than dipping in and out.

Laughton, R. (1966), *TV Graphics*, London: Studio Vista.
An old book, which may be hard to find, but one of the first to begin to examine TV graphics. Many of the conventions of motion design have been inherited from the early days of TV graphics, and this book reveals what some of those conventions are.

Meyer, T. and C. Meyer, (2010), *Creating Motion Graphics with After Effects: Essential and Advanced Techniques*, 5th edn, Waltham, Mass.: Focal Press.
A very useful and detailed extension to the After Effects software manual. It explains the general concepts but also addresses the specific terminology of menus within After Effects. Implementable examples are included. The technical vocabulary may be more accessible if you are already acquainted with After Effects.

Nielsen, D. and K. Hartmann (2005), *Inspired: How Creative People Think, Work and Find Inspiration*, Amsterdam: BIS.
Like Brereton's *Sketchbooks*, this reveals some of the creative habits and thought processes of designers in a variety of different fields.

Shaughnessy, A. (2010), *How To Be a Graphic Designer Without Losing Your Soul*, London: Laurence King.
A helpful and straight-talking guidebook for young designers who want to earn a living doing meaningful work, but want to avoid becoming a drone working on soulless projects.

Taylor, A. (2010), *Design Essentials for the Motion Media Artist: A Practical Guide to Principles & Techniques*, Waltham, Mass.: Focal Press.
A highly motivational book that describes the tools, the soft skills, and the literacies that an animator/motion designer requires. It is something of a manifesto for the promotion of the craft of drawing. There are many chapters relating to the design of images and the visual elements that comprise an image, although there is less discussion of time and motion.

Vineyard, J. (1999), *Setting Up Your Shots: Great Camera Moves Every Filmmaker Should Know*, Studio City, CA: Michael Wiese Productions.
A directory of visual guides that reveals how to set up different types of camera angles and camera movements. The book uses familiar examples to explain why you might need to use certain types of complex shots.

Williams, R. (2004), *The Non-designer's Design Book: Design and Typographic Principles for the Visual Novice*, 2nd edn, Berkeley: Peachpit.
A crucial introduction to design and typography. An essential book for anybody involved in visual media. Typographer Robin Williams distills the dark art of design down to four easy-to-remember and easy-to-apply principles.

Woolman, M. and J. Bellantoni (2000), *Moving Type: Designing for Time and Space*, Hove: RotoVision.
This book is out of print, but it may be worth searching online bookshops for an old copy. The book is in two parts: The first is very rich in useful terminology relating to type and the planning of motion. The second is a showcase of motion type used for eclectic purposes. The taxonomy section at the beginning provides helpful terms for discussing and articulating your intentions for type and motion.

Websites

aescripts.com
Aescripts + Aeplugins is a widely used network for high-quality plugins and tutorials. Despite the name, it is not solely concerned with After Effects, but has information, tutorials, and downloads for many pieces of software.

cgi.tutsplus.com
Well used site with thousands of free tutorials on all aspects of motion graphics as well as full subscription-based courses.

www.creativecow.net
Creative Cow is huge and describes itself as the peer-to-peer support community for media production professionals. It covers all aspects of media but has a large and active group dedicated to motion graphics.

www.lynda.com/Motion-Graphics -training-tutorials/84-0.html
Lynda.com provides easy-to-follow, high-quality tutorials on many topics. The service works on a subscription basis but has a huge following.

motionanddesign.net
A good collection of easy-to-follow tutorials on Adobe After Effects and Cinema 4D.

motiongraphicscollective.com
Described as a "publishing platform, for VFX artists and motion designers," this website features a constantly changing gallery of inspirational work. Users can upload their own projects for inclusion.

motiongraphics.nu
A regularly updated and curated gallery of motion design works. Featuring many company showreels, it offers plenty of inspiration.

motionographer.com
Since 2006, Motionographer has showcased outstanding work in motion design, animation, and digital storytelling.

www.motionserved.com
Another regularly updated and curated gallery of motion design works.

motionspire.com
A collection of inspiring motion graphics.

motionworks.net
Motionworks provides high-quality learning resources through tutorials, experiments, and blogs. Site creator John Dickinson also produces a series of short video shows with interviews and articles related to motion graphics.

tv.adobe.com
Adobe TV has high-quality tutorials and support on the Adobe suite of products.

www.videocopilot.net/tutorials/ motion_graphics
Massive site of tutorials, information, and high-quality plugin software for purchase. Many of the tutorials are delivered by site creator and video post-production expert Andrew Kramer.

vimeo.com/channels/motionsoup
vimeo.com/channels/pmg
vimeo.com/channels/motionographer
vimeo.com/channels/ awesomemotiongraphics
vimeo.com/channels/kinetictypography
Just a few of the many excellent and inspiring channels around the subject of motion graphics to be found on Vimeo.

INDEX

PICTURE CREDITS

Cover Image
The Zone images courtesy of Tendril, www.tendril.ca.

Contents
Page 4: *Hannibal* images, *THE SHELL/Copelia* images, and *Great Expectations* images courtesy of Momoco, www.momoco.co.uk.

Accuhealth images courtesy of Bark and Bite, www.barkandbite.com.

Page 5: Amazon Kindle – Paper and Pen images © 2014 Lucas Zanotto/Troublemakers.tv, www.lucaszanotto.com; troublemakers.tv.

Luther image courtesy of Momoco, www.momoco.co.uk.

Other images courtesy of Tendril, www.tendril.ca.

Introduction
Page 7: *Luther* images courtesy of Momoco, www.momoco.co.uk.

Strike Suit Zero images © 2012 Born Ready Games. Images courtesy of Territory, www.territorystudio.com.

Page 9: Images from *Killzone™ Mercenary* for PSVITA™ © 2013 Sony Computer Entertainment Europe. Images courtesy of Territory, www.territorystudio.com.

Page 11: RSA Animate Images © Cognitive Media Ltd, www.wearecognitive.com.

Pages 12–13: ChilliBeans images courtesy of Bark and Bite, www.barkandbite.com.

Page 15: *Hannibal* images courtesy of Momoco, www.momoco.co.uk.

Chapter One
Page 17: Amazon Kindle – Paper and Pen images © 2014 Lucas Zanotto/Troublemakers.tv, www.lucaszanotto.com; troublemakers.tv.

Page 27: Adobe product screenshot reprinted with permission from Adobe Systems Incorporated.

Page 31: Natron screenshot reprinted with permission from Alexandre Gauthier-Foichat, natron.inria.fr.

Page 33: Images © Getty Images, www.gettyimages.co.uk.

Page 35: Appalachian Trail film images courtesy of Meg Soro, www.megsoro.com.

Page 37: Amazon Kindle – Paper and Pen images © 2014 Lucas Zanotto/Troublemakers.tv, www.lucaszanotto.com; troublemakers.tv.

Page 39: Image © Getty Images, www.gettyimages.co.uk.

Page 41: *Fortitude* images courtesy of Momoco, www.momoco.co.uk.

Page 42: *THE SHELL/Copelia* images courtesy of Momoco, www.momoco.co.uk.

Chapter Two
Page 49: William Hill *Las Vegas* images courtesy of Bark and Bite, www.barkandbite.com.

Pages 52–53: Open Text images courtesy of Tendril, www.tendril.ca.

Page 55: Accuhealth images courtesy of Bark and Bite, www.barkandbite.com.

Pages 58–59: *Great Expectations* images courtesy of Momoco, www.momoco.co.uk.

Page 65: Missguided images courtesy of Bark and Bite, www.barkandbite.com.

Pages 72–73: To Do List images © Yaniv Fridman and Daniel Luna. Images courtesy of Tendril, www.tendril.ca.

Pages: 74–75: *The Overfishing of the Ocean* images © Uli Streckenbach, www.uhsless.de.

Pages 76–77: *F-Gases* images © Uli Streckenbach, www.uhsless.de.

Chapter Three
Page 79: *The Zone* images courtesy of Tendril, www.tendril.ca.

Page 83: *Let's Talk about Soil* images © Uli Streckenbach. Images courtesy of Uli Streckenbach/Ronny Schmidt, www.uhsless.de.

Page 84: *Preston Bus Station* images courtesy of Richard Johnson.

Pages 86–87: *Bank of Arizona* images courtesy of Joe Fellows, Make Productions, www.makeproductions.co.uk.

Pages 88–89: PESETA images © Uli Streckenbach. Images courtesy of Uli Streckenbach/Robert Pohle, www.uhsless.de.

Page 92: Images courtesy of
Kim Langstroth.

Pages 96, 97 and 99: Images courtesy
of Joe Fellows, Make Productions,
www.makeproductions.co.uk.

Chapter Four
Page 101: *Living Moments* images
courtesy of Paul Trillo, http://paultrillo
.com.

Page 105: *Dance (RED) Save Lives*
images courtesy of Paul Trillo,
http://paultrillo.com.

Page 111: Brooklyn Brewery images
courtesy of Paul Trillo, http://paultrillo
.com.

Page 113: *Living Moments* images
courtesy of Paul Trillo, http://paultrillo
.com.

Page 115: *The Zone* images courtesy
of Tendril, www.tendril.ca.

Chapter Five
Page 119: *United Way* images courtesy
of Joe Fellows, Make Productions,
www.makeproductions.co.uk.

Page 121: Dorset Cereal images courtesy
of Nexus, www.nexusproductions.com.

Pages 128–129: Images from *Heroes
and Generals* © 2014 Reto-Moto Aps.
Images courtesy of Territory,
www.territorystudio.com.

Pages 132–133: *THE SHELL/Copelia*
images courtesy of Momoco,
www.momoco.co.uk.

Pages 134–135: *Strike Suit Zero* images
© 2012 Born Ready Games.
Images courtesy of Territory,
www.territorystudio.com.

Pages 136–139: Images courtesy of
Max Jauga, www.maximusworks.com.

Chapter Six
Page 147: Adobe product screenshot
reprinted with permission from
Adobe Systems Incorporated.

Chapter Seven
Page 153: Image courtesy of
Wash Design, wash-design.co.uk.

Pages 156–157: Images courtesy
of Johnny Hardstaff,
www.johnnyhardstaff.com.

Pages 159–161: Images courtesy
of Paul Greer.

Pages 166–167: Images courtesy
of The Neighbourhood,
www.the-neighbourhood.com.

Chapter Eight
Page 169: Path Messaging images
courtesy of Paul Trillo, http://paultrillo
.com.

Page 175: Dorset Cereal images courtesy
of Nexus, www.nexusproductions.com.

Page 176: Image © Getty Images,
www.gettyimages.co.uk.

Page 178: Free Music Archive website
screenshot reprinted with permission
from The Free Music Archive,
freemusicarchive.org.

Pages 180–182: Images courtesy
of Tendril, www.tendril.ca.

All reasonable attempts have been made
to trace, clear, and credit the copyright
holders of the images reproduced in the
book. However, if any credits have been
inadvertently omitted, the publisher will
endeavour to incorporate amendments
in future editions.

ACKNOWLEDGMENTS

Ian and Peter would like to thank the following people for their help and support in the writing of this book:

Michelle, Mabel, and Jacob Beare
Nic Benns
Christopher Black
Jennifer Bonnar
Deborah, Molly, and Owen Crook
Miriam Davey
Roger Fawcett-Tang
Joe Fellows
Alexandre Gauthier
Francois "Coyhot" Grassard
Paul Greer
Johnny Hardstaff
Rachel Hartley
Claire Henry
Max Jauga
Georgia Kennedy
Kim Langstroth
Robert Phelps
David Reiverson
Dana Richards
David Sheldon-Hicks
Meg Soro
Uli Henrik Streckenbach
Paul Trillo
Andy Walmsley
Matthew White
Molly Willows
Caroline Wood
Samantha Yetunde
Lucas Zanotto

The publishers would like to thank:

Julia DeArriba-Montgomery
Peter Hriso
Alex Jukes
João Paulo Amaral Schlittler